PLANT-BASED DIET IN :

BUILD HEALTHY HABITS FOR LIFE WITH DELICIOUS

PLANT-BASED RECIPES AND MEAL PLAN

Table of Contents

Introduction

What Is a Plant-Based Diet?

A plant-based diet is a type of diet that is made up of mostly or entirely of food that comes from plants, including fruits, vegetables, seeds, grains, legumes, and nuts. This type of diet contains little or no animal products.

People decide to start a plant-based diet for various reasons, including health, concerns about animal treatment, environmental concerns, and some because of social pressure or taste.

Plant-based based diets can be seen as a perfect blend of health and kindness to animal rights, the human body, and the environment. If you finally make up your mind to start a plant-based diet and to avoid eating foods like meat, eggs, and dairy but choose to live instead of legumes, vegetables, seeds, nuts, fruits, and beans, then consider adding these to your diet to help keep you strong and healthy.

Benefits

> **Lowers blood pressure**

Plant-based dieting helps lower one's blood pressure due to the higher presence of potassium in most plant-based foods.

> **Prevents and fights off chronic diseases**

Research has shown that in a community or society where most people maintain a plant-based lifestyle, the rate of obesity, cancer, and diabetes is often lower than in a society where the people are mostly consumers of meat.

> **Lowers cholesterol**

Since plants do not contain cholesterol, living a plant-based lifestyle will help you reduce the level of cholesterol stored in your body. This helps you in the long run to reduce the risk of heart disease.

> ➢ **Reduces blood sugar levels**

Experts have scientifically proven that plants contain many fibers that help slow down the absorption of sugar into the bloodstream. These fibers also help keep you feeling great for a longer period as they balance the blood cortisol levels, thereby reducing stress.

> ➢ **Improved energy and vitality**

Consuming more green and leafy veggies and fruits helps one to feel more energized and strong.

> ➢ **Induces better quality sleep**

Good food often equates to better sleep at night. When you eat and nourish the body during the day with sumptuous plant-based meals regularly, you will notice that the quality of your sleep at night will improve.

> ➢ **Weight loss**

It is often recommended for individuals seeking to watch their weight or cut down on their body weight to eating more plant-based meals. Eating whole plant-based meals helps you easily cut down on your excess weight while maintaining healthy body weight.

> ➢ **Effective for cancer patients**

Plant-based foods are believed to be effective against cancer because they come fully packed with phytonutrients. These chemicals are domicile in plants, and they help to prevent or fight against diseases and infections.

> ➢ **Heart disease and hypertension**

To properly take care of your heart, the best route to follow is the plant-based way of eating. This is a better option since animal-based foods are often loaded with cholesterol and fat, and these are built up in the arteries, thereby causing high blood pressure or risk of having heart disease.

> ➢ **Gastrointestinal illnesses**

Another great benefit of plant-based dieting is the wide variety of help it can render to people suffering from different types of gastrointestinal conditions. A Plant-based diet that is high in vitamins, minerals, and fiber can help prevent the inception and progression of these frequent diseases.

Foods to Eat

From steak to bacon and eggs for dinner, animal-based meals are what a lot of people focus on. When starting a plant-based diet, your meal must be based around plant-based foods, and consumption of animal-based foods should be limited. This means that animal-based foods like poultry, dairy, meat, seafood, and eggs shouldn't be the main focus of your meal; instead, they can be used as a complement to plant-based meals.

When you finally decide to follow a plant-based diet, below is a list of foods you can consume:

- **Vegetables:** Carrots, kale, peppers, tomatoes, spinach, asparagus, broccoli, cauliflower, etc.

- **Whole Grains:** Rolled oats, quinoa, brown rice, brown rice pasta, faro, etc.

- Fruit: Pears, bananas, apples, berries, peaches, mangoes, pineapples, etc.

- **Legumes:** Chickpeas, peas, black beans, peanuts, lentils, etc.

- **Starchy Vegetables:** Sweet potatoes, butternut squash, potatoes, etc.

- **Nuts, Seeds, and Nut Butters:** Tahini, almonds, sunflower seeds, macadamia nuts, natural peanut butter, pumpkin seeds, etc.

- **Healthy Fats:** Olive oil, unsweetened coconut, avocados, coconut oil, etc.

- **Condiments:** Mustard, soy sauce, lemon juice, salsa, nutritional yeast, vinegar, etc.

- **Plant-based Protein:** Tempeh, Tofu, plant-based protein sources, etc.

- **Unsweetened Plant-based Milk:** Almond milk, cashew milk, coconut milk, etc.

- **Spices, Seasonings, and Herbs**: Rosemary, turmeric, black pepper, basil, curry, salt, etc.

- **Beverages:** Sparkling water, tea, coffee, etc.

Foods You Should Minimize

Although you can choose to include healthy animal foods in your plant-based diet plan, the following foods should be consumed in small quantities.

- Eggs
- Dairy
- Game meats
- Beef
- Seafood
- Pork
- Poultry
- Lamb

If you decide to supplement your plant-based diet with animal foods, ensure you select quality products from the store or buy them from local farmers.

- **Dairy:** Always select organic dairy foods from pasture-raised animals.
- **Poultry:** Free-range and organic whenever possible.
- **Seafood:** Always choose wild-caught, which is from sustainable fisheries.
- **Eggs:** Always select pasture-raised eggs whenever possible.
- **Pork and Beef:** Always select grass-fed or pastured when possible.

Foods to Avoid

- **Fast Food:** Hotdogs, French fries, cheeseburgers, chicken nuggets, etc.

- **Processed Animal Foods:** Lunch meats, beef jerky, bacon, sausage, etc.

- **Refined Grains:** Bagels, white pasta, white rice, white bread, etc.

- **Added Sugars and Sweets:** Soda, sugary cereals, pastries, candy, cookies, table sugar, sweet tea, etc.

- **Convenience and Packed Foods:** Cereal bars, chips, frozen dinners, crackers, etc.

Chapter 1. Breakfast

1. Apple Cinnamon Muffins

Preparation Time: 5-15 minutes
Cooking Time: 40 minutes
Servings: 4
Ingredients:
For the muffins:

- 1 flax seed powder + 3 tbsp water
- 1 ½ cups whole-wheat flour
- ¾ cup pure date sugar
- 2 tsp baking powder
- ¼ tsp salt
- 1 tsp cinnamon powder
- 1/3 cup melted plant butter
- 1/3 cup flax milk
- 2 apples, peeled, cored, and chopped

For topping:

- 1/3 cup whole-wheat flour
- ½ cup pure date sugar
- ½ cup cold plant butter, cubed
- 1 ½ tsp cinnamon powder

Directions:

1. Preheat oven to 400°F and grease 6 muffin cups with cooking spray. In a bowl, mix the flax seed powder with water and allow thickening for 5 minutes to make the flax egg.
2. In a medium bowl, mix the flour, date sugar, baking powder, salt, and cinnamon powder. Whisk in the butter, flax egg, flax milk, and then fold in the apples. Fill the muffin cups two-thirds way up with the batter.
3. In a small bowl, mix the remaining flour, date sugar, cold butter, and cinnamon powder.

Sprinkle the mixture on the muffin batter. Bake for 20 minutes. Remove the muffins onto a wire rack, allow cooling, and serve warm.

Nutrition:

- Calories 1133
- Fats 74.9 g
- Carbs 104.3 g
- Protein 18 g

2. Mixed Berry Walnut Yogurt

Preparation Time: 5-15 minutes
Cooking Time: 10 minutes
Servings: 4
Ingredients:

- 4 cups almond milk Dairy-Free yogurt, cold
- 2 tbsp pure malt syrup
- 2 cups mixed berries, halved or chopped
- ¼ cup chopped toasted walnuts

Directions:

1. In a medium bowl, mix the yogurt and malt syrup until well-combined. Divide the mixture into 4 breakfast bowls.
2. Top with the berries and walnuts.
3. Enjoy immediately.

Nutrition:

- Calories 326
- Fats 14.3 g
- Carbs 38.3 g
- Protein 12.5 g

3. Orange Butter Crepes

Preparation Time: 5-15 minutes
Cooking Time: 30 minutes
Servings: 4
Ingredients:

- 2 tbsp flax seed powder + 6 tbsp water
- 1 tsp vanilla extract
- 1 tsp pure date sugar
- ¼ tsp salt
- 2 cups almond flour
- 1½ cups oat milk
- ½ cup melted plant butter
- 3 tbsp fresh orange juice
- 3 tbsp plant butter for frying

Directions:

1. In a medium bowl, mix the flax seed powder with 1 cup water and allow thickening for 5 minutes to make the flax egg. Whisk in the vanilla, date sugar, and salt.
2. Pour in a quarter cup of almond flour and whisk, then a quarter cup of oat milk, and mix until no lumps remain. Repeat the mixing process with the remaining almond flour and almond milk in the same quantities until exhausted.
3. Mix in the plant butter, orange juice, and half of the water until the mixture is runny like that of pancakes. Add the remaining water until the mixture is lighter. Brush a large non-stick skillet with some butter and place over medium heat to melt.
4. Pour 1 tablespoon of the batter into the pan and swirl the skillet quickly and all around to coat the pan with the batter. Cook until the batter is dry and golden brown beneath, about 30 seconds.
5. Use a spatula to carefully flip the crepe and cook the other side until golden brown too. Fold the crepe onto a plate and set it aside. Repeat making more crepes with the remaining batter until exhausted. Drizzle some maple syrup on the crepes and serve.

Nutrition:

- Calories 379
- Fats 35.6 g
- Carbs 14.8 g
- Protein 5.6 g

4. Creole Tofu Scramble

Preparation Time: 5-15 minutes
Cooking Time: 20 minutes
Servings: 4
Ingredients:

- 2 tbsp plant butter, for frying
- 1 (14 oz) pack firm tofu, pressed and crumbled
- 1 medium red bell pepper, deseeded and chopped
- 1 medium green bell pepper, deseeded and chopped
- 1 tomato, finely chopped
- 2 tbsp chopped fresh green onions
- Salt and black pepper to taste

- 1 tsp turmeric powder
- 1 tsp Creole seasoning
- ½ cup chopped baby kale
- ¼ cup grated plant-based Parmesan cheese

Directions:
1. Melt the plant butter in a large skillet over medium heat and add the tofu. Cook with occasional stirring until the tofu is light golden brown while making sure not to break the tofu into tiny bits but to have scrambled egg resemblance, 5 minutes.
2. Stir in the bell peppers, tomato, green onions, salt, black pepper, turmeric powder, and Creole seasoning. Sauté until the vegetables soften, 5 minutes.
3. Mix in the kale to wilt, 3 minutes and then, half of the plant-based Parmesan cheese. Allow melting for 1 to 2 minutes and then turn the heat off.
4. Dish the food, top with the remaining cheese, and serve warm.

Nutrition:
- Calories 258
- Fats 15.9 g
- Carbs 12.8 g
- Protein 20.7 g

5.   Savory   Breakfast Salad

Preparation Time: 15-30 minutes
Cooking Time: 20 minutes
Servings: 2
Ingredients:
- 2 small Sweet potatoes
- 1 pinch Salt and pepper:

- 1 tbsp Coconut oil

For the Dressing:
- 3 tbsp Lemon juice
- 1 pinch each Salt and pepper
- 1 tbsp Extra virgin olive oil

For the Salad:
- 4 cups mixed greens

For Servings:
- 4 tbsp Hummus
- 1 cup Blueberries
- 1 medium ripe avocado
- Fresh chopped parsley
- 2 tbsp Hemp seeds

Directions:
1. Take a large skillet and apply gentle heat
2. Add sweet potatoes, coat them with salt and pepper and pour some oil
3. Cook till sweet potatoes turns browns
4. Take a bowl and mix lemon juice, salt, and pepper
5. Add salad, sweet potatoes, and the serving together
6. Mix well and dress and serve

Nutrition:
- Carbs 57.6 g
- Protein 7.5 g
- Calories 37.6 g
- Calories 523

6. Almond Plum Oats Overnight

Preparation Time: 15-30 minutes
Cooking Time: 10 minutes plus overnight
Servings: 2
Ingredients:

- 60 g Rolled oats
- 3 Plums ripe and chopped
- 300 ml Almond milk
- 1 tbsp Chia seeds
- Nutmeg (a pinch)
- A few drops of Vanilla extract
- 1 tbsp Whole almonds roughly chopped

Directions:

1. Add oats, nutmeg, vanilla extract, almond milk, and chia seeds to a bowl and mix well
2. Add in cubed plums and cover and place in the fridge for a night
3. Mix the oats well the next morning and add into the serving bowl
4. Serve with your favorite toppings

Nutrition:

- Carbs 24.7 g
- Protein 9.5 g
- Calories 10.8 g
- Calories 248

7. Guacamole

Preparation Time: 15-30 minutes
Cooking Time: 15 minutes
Servings: 4
Ingredients:

- 3 ripe Avocados
- 1 Fresh jalapeño chilies, finely chopped
- ¼ Red onion, finely chopped
- 2 Tomatoes small diced
- ½ Garlic crushed
- 2 tbsp Lime juice
- ¼ cup Coriander finely chopped
- 1 tsp Sea salt
- Plain tortilla chips to serve

Directions:

1. Take a bowl and add onion, chilies, garlic and lime juice
2. Add salt from the top, mix and leave for 5 minutes
3. Add the remaining ingredient and mash using a fork
4. Add avocados, mix and serve with plain tortilla chips

Nutrition:

- Carbs 21.7 g
- Protein 5.2 g
- Calories 7.1 g
- Calories 256

8. High Protein Toast

Preparation Time: 15-30 minutes
Cooking Time: 15 minutes
Servings: 2
Ingredients:
- 1 White bean, drained and rinsed
- ½ cup Cashew cream
- 1 ½ tbsp Miso paste
- 1 tsp toasted sesame oil
- 1 tbsp Sesame seeds
- 1 Spring onion, finely sliced
- Lemon: 1 half for the juice and half wedged to serve
- 4 slices Rye bread, toasted

Directions:
1. In a bowl, add sesame oil, white beans, miso, cashew cream, and lemon juice and mash using a potato masher
2. Make a spread
3. Spread it on a toast and top with spring onions and sesame seeds
4. Serve with lemon wedges

Nutrition:
- Carbs 44.05 g
- Protein 14.05 g
- Calories 9.25 g
- Calories 332

9. Berry Compote Pancakes

Preparation Time: 15-30 minutes
Cooking Time: 30 minutes
Servings: 2
Ingredients:
- 200 g Mixed frozen berries
- 140 g Plain flour
- 140 ml Unsweetened almond milk
- 1 tbsp Icing sugar
- 1 tbsp Lemon juice
- 2 tsp Baking powder
- Vanilla extract: a dash
- Salt: a pinch
- 2 tbsp Caster sugar
- ½ tbsp Vegetable oil

Directions:
1. Take a small pan and add berries, lemon juice, and icing sugar
2. Cook the mixture for 10 minutes to give it a saucy texture and set aside
3. Take a bowl and add caster sugar, flour, baking powder, and salt and mix well
4. Add in almond milk and vanilla and combine well to make a batter
5. Take a non-stick pan, and heat 2 teaspoons of oil in it and spread it over the whole surface
6. Add ¼ cup of the batter to the pan and cook each side for 3-4 minutes
7. Serve with compote

Nutrition:
- Carbs 92 g
- Protein 9.4 g
- Calories 5.2 g
- Calories 463

10. Southwest Breakfast Bowl

Preparation Time: 15-30 minutes
Cooking Time: 15 minutes
Servings: 1
Ingredients:

- 1 cup Mushrooms, sliced
- ½ cup Chopped cilantro
- 1 tsp Chili powder
- 1/2 diced Red pepper
- 1 cup Zucchini, diced
- 1/2 cup Green onion, chopped
- 1/2 cup Onion
- Vegan sausage: 1 sliced
- 1 tsp Garlic powder
- 1 tsp Paprika
- 1/2 tsp Cumin
- Salt and pepper: as per your taste
- Avocado: for topping

Directions:

1. Put everything in a bowl and apply gentle heat until vegetables turn brown
2. Pour some pepper and salt as you like and serve with your favorite toppings

Nutrition:

- Carbs 31.6 g
- Protein 33.8 g
- Calories 12.2 g
- Calories 361

11. Vegan Muffins Breakfast Sandwich

Preparation Time: 15-30 minutes
Cooking Time: 20 minutes
Servings: 2
Ingredients:

- 3-4 tablespoons Romesco Sauce
- ½ cup Fresh baby spinach
- 2 Tofu Scramble
- 2 Vegan English muffins
- ½ Avocado, peeled and sliced
- 1 Sliced fresh tomato

Directions:

1. In the oven, toast one English muffin
2. Half the muffin and spread romesco sauce
3. Paste spinach to one side, tailed by avocado slices
4. Have warm tofu followed by a tomato slice
5. Place the other muffin half onto the preceding one

Nutrition:

- Carbs 18 g
- Protein 12 g
- Calories 14 g
- Calories 276

12. Almond Waffles with Cranberries

Preparation Time: 5-15 minutes
Cooking Time: 20 minutes
Servings: 4
Ingredients:
- 2 tbsp flax seed powder + 6 tbsp water
- 2/3 cup almond flour
- 2 ½ tsp baking powder
- A pinch salt
- 1 ½ cups almond milk
- 2 tbsp plant butter
- 1 cup fresh almond butter
- 2 tbsp pure maple syrup
- 1 tsp fresh lemon juice

Directions:
1. In a medium bowl, mix the flax seed powder with water and allow soaking for 5 minutes.
2. Add the almond flour, baking powder, salt, and almond milk. Mix until well combined.
3. Preheat a waffle iron and brush with some plant butter. Pour in a quarter cup of the batter, close the iron and cook until the waffles are golden and crisp, 2 to 3 minutes.
4. Transfer the waffles to a plate and make more waffles using the same process and ingredient proportions.
5. Meanwhile, in a medium bowl, mix the almond butter with maple syrup and lemon juice. Serve the waffles, spread the top with the almond-lemon mixture, and serve.

Nutrition:
- Calories 533
- Fats 53 g
- Carbs 16.7 g
- Protein 1.2 g

13. Chickpea Omelet with Spinach and Mushrooms

Preparation Time: 5-15 minutes
Cooking Time: 25 minutes
Servings: 4
Ingredients:
- 1 cup chickpea flour
- ½ tsp onion powder
- ½ tsp garlic powder
- ¼ tsp white pepper
- ¼ tsp black pepper
- 1/3 cup nutritional yeast
- ½ tsp baking soda
- 1 small green bell pepper, deseeded and chopped
- 3 scallions, chopped

- 1 cup sautéed sliced white button mushrooms
- ½ cup chopped fresh spinach
- 1 cup halved cherry tomatoes for serving
- 1 tbsp fresh parsley leaves

Directions:
1. In a medium bowl, mix the chickpea flour, onion powder, garlic powder, white pepper, black pepper, nutritional yeast, and baking soda until well combined.
2. Heat a medium skillet over medium heat and add a quarter of the batter. Swirl the pan to spread the batter across the pan. Scatter a quarter each of the bell pepper, scallions, mushrooms, and spinach on top, and cook until the bottom part of the omelet sets and is golden brown, 1 to 2 minutes. Carefully, flip the omelet and cook the other side until set and golden brown.
3. Transfer the omelet to a plate and make the remaining omelets using the remaining batter in the same proportions.
4. Serve the omelet with the tomatoes and garnish with the parsley leaves. Serve.

Nutrition:
- Calories 147
- Fats 1.8 g
- Carbs 21.3 g
- Protein 11.6 g

14. Sweet Coconut Raspberry Pancakes

Preparation Time: 5-15 minutes
Cooking Time: 25 minutes
Servings: 4
Ingredients:
- 2 tbsp flax seed powder + 6 tbsp water
- ½ cup coconut milk
- ¼ cup fresh raspberries, mashed
- ½ cup oat flour
- 1 tsp baking soda
- A pinch salt
- 1 tbsp coconut sugar
- 2 tbsp pure date syrup
- ½ tsp cinnamon powder
- 2 tbsp unsweetened coconut flakes
- 2 tsp plant butter
- Fresh raspberries for garnishing

Directions:
1. In a medium bowl, mix the flax seed powder with the water and allow thickening for 5 minutes.
2. Mix in the coconut milk and raspberries.
3. Add the oat flour, baking soda, salt, coconut sugar, date syrup, and cinnamon powder. Fold in the coconut flakes until well combined.
4. Working in batches, melt a quarter of the butter in a non-stick skillet and add ¼ cup of the batter. Cook until set beneath and golden brown, 2 minutes. Flip the pancake and cook on the other side until set and golden brown, 2 minutes. Transfer to a plate and make the remaining pancakes using the rest of the ingredients in the same proportions.
5. Garnish the pancakes with some raspberries and serve warm!

Nutrition:
- Calories 412
- Fats 28.3 g
- Carbs 33.7 g
- Protein 7.6 g

15.   Pumpkin-Pistachio Tea Cake

Preparation Time: 5-15 minutes
Cooking Time: 70 minutes
Servings: 4
Ingredients:

- 2 tbsp flaxseed powder + 6 tbsp water
- 3 tbsp vegetable oil
- ¾ cup canned unsweetened pumpkin puree
- ½ cup pure corn syrup
- 3 tbsp pure date sugar
- 1 ½ cups whole-wheat flour
- ½ tsp cinnamon powder
- ½ tsp baking powder
- ¼ tsp cloves powder
- ½ tsp allspice powder
- ½ tsp nutmeg powder
- A pinch salt
- 2 tbsp chopped pistachios

Directions:

1. Preheat the oven to 350°F and lightly coat an 8 x 4-inch loaf pan with cooking spray. In a medium bowl, mix the flax seed powder with water and allow thickening for 5 minutes to make the flax egg.
2. In a bowl, whisk the vegetable oil, pumpkin puree, corn syrup, date sugar, and flax egg. In another bowl, mix the flour, cinnamon powder, baking powder, cloves powder, allspice powder, nutmeg powder and salt. Add this mixture to the wet batter and mix until well combined.
3. Pour the batter into the loaf pan, sprinkle the pistachios on top, and gently press the nuts onto the batter to stick.
4. Bake in the oven for 50 to 55 minutes or until a toothpick inserted into the cake comes out clean. Remove the cake onto a wire rack, allow cooling, slice, and serve.

Nutrition:

- Calories 330
- Fats 13.2 g
- Carbs 50.1 g
- Protein 7 g

16. Carrot and Chocolate Bread

Preparation Time: 5-15 minutes
Cooking Time: 75 minutes
Servings: 4
Ingredients:
For the dry mix:

- 1 ½ cup whole-wheat flour
- ¼ cup almond flour
- ¼ tsp salt
- ¼ tsp cloves powder
- ¼ tsp cayenne pepper
- 1 tbsp cinnamon powder
- ½ tsp nutmeg powder
- ½ tsp baking soda
- 1 ½ tsp baking powder

For the wet batter:

- 2 tbsp flax seed powder + 6 tbsp water

- ½ cup pure date sugar
- ¼ cup pure maple syrup
- ¾ tsp almond extract
- 1 tbsp grated lemon zest
- ½ cup unsweetened applesauce
- ¼ cup olive oil

For folding into the batter:
- 4 carrots, shredded
- 3 tbsp unsweetened chocolate chips
- 2/3 cup black raisins

Directions:
1. Preheat the oven to 375°F and line an 8x4 loaf tin with baking paper.
2. In a large bowl, mix all the flour, salt, cloves powder, cayenne pepper, cinnamon powder, nutmeg powder, baking soda, and baking powder.
3. In another bowl, mix the flaxseed powder, water, and allow thickening for 5 minutes. Mix in the date sugar, maple syrup, almond extract, lemon zest, applesauce, and olive oil.
4. Combine both mixtures until smooth and fold in the carrots, chocolate chips, and raisins.
5. Pour the mixture into a loaf pan and bake in the oven until golden brown on top or a toothpick inserted into the bread comes out clean, 45 to 60 minutes.
6. Remove from the oven, transfer the bread onto a wire rack to cool, slice, and serve.

Nutrition:
- Calories 524
- Fats 15.8 g
- Carbs 94.3 g
- Protein 7.9 g

17. Nectarine Chia Pudding

Preparation Time: 5-15 minutes
Cooking Time: 5 minutes + 4 hour refrigeration
Servings: 4
Ingredients:
- 1 cup coconut milk
- ½ tsp vanilla extract
- 3 tbsp chia seeds
- ½ cup granola
- 2/3 cup chopped sweet nectarine

Directions:
1. In a medium bowl, mix the coconut milk, vanilla, and chia seeds until well combined.
2. Divide the mixture between 4 breakfast cups and refrigerate for at least 4 hours to allow the mixture to gel.
3. After, top with granola and nectarine. Enjoy immediately.

Nutrition:
- Calories 72
- Fats 3.4 g
- Carbs 7.8 g
- Protein 2.6 g

18. Pineapple French Toasts

Preparation Time: 5-15 minutes
Cooking Time: 55 minutes
Servings: 4
Ingredients:
- 2 tbsp flax seed powder + 6 tbsp water
- 1 ½ cups unsweetened almond milk
- ½ cup almond flour
- 2 tbsp pure maple syrup + extra for drizzling
- 2 pinches salt

- ½ tbsp cinnamon powder
- ½ tsp fresh lemon zest
- 1 tbsp fresh pineapple juice
- 8 whole-grain bread slices

Directions:
1. Preheat the oven to 400°F and lightly grease a toasting rack with olive oil. Set aside.
2. In a medium bowl, mix the flax seed powder with water and allow thickening for 5 to 10 minutes.
3. Whisk in the almond milk, almond flour, maple syrup, salt, cinnamon powder, lemon zest, and pineapple juice.
4. Soak the bread on both sides in the almond milk mixture and allow sitting on a plate for 2 to 3 minutes.
5. Heat a large skillet over medium heat and place the bread in the pan. Cook until golden brown on the bottom side. Flip the bread and cook further until golden brown on the other side, 4 minutes in total.
6. Transfer to a plate, drizzle some maple syrup on top and serve immediately.

Nutrition:
- Calories 294
- Fats 4.7 g
- Carbs 52.0 g
- Protein 11.6 g

19. Pimiento Cheese Breakfast Biscuits

Preparation Time: 5-15 minutes
Cooking Time: 30 minutes
Servings: 4
Ingredients:
- 2 cups whole-wheat flour
- 2 tsp baking powder
- 1 tsp salt
- ½ tsp baking soda
- ½ tsp garlic powder
- ¼ tsp black pepper
- ¼ cup unsalted plant butter, cold and cut into 1/2-inch cubes
- ¾ cup coconut milk
- 1 cup shredded cashew cheese
- 1 (4 oz) jar chopped pimientos, well-drained
- 1 tbsp melted unsalted plant butter

Directions:
1. Preheat the oven to 450°F and line a baking sheet with parchment paper. Set aside. In a medium bowl, mix the flour, baking powder, salt, baking soda, garlic powder, and black pepper. Add the cold butter using a hand mixer until the mixture is the size of small peas.
2. Pour in ¾ of the coconut milk and continue whisking. Continue adding the remaining coconut milk, a tablespoonful at a time, until dough forms.
3. Mix in the cashew cheese and pimientos. (If the dough is too wet to handle, mix in a little bit more flour until it is manageable). Place the dough on a lightly floured surface and flatten the dough into ½-inch thickness.
4. Use a 2 ½-inch round cutter to cut out biscuits' pieces from the dough. Gather, re-roll the dough once and continue cutting out biscuits. Arrange the biscuits on the prepared pan and brush the tops with the melted butter. Bake for 12-14 minutes, or until the biscuits are golden brown. Cool and serve.

Nutrition:
- Calories 1009
- Fats 71.8 g
- Carbs 74.8 g
- Protein 24.5 g

20. Raspberry Raisin Muffins with Orange Glaze

Preparation Time: 5-15 minutes
Cooking Time: 40 minutes
Servings: 4
Ingredients:
For the muffins:
- 2 tbsp flax seed powder + 6 tbsp water
- 2 cups whole-wheat flour
- 1½ tsp baking powder
- A pinch salt
- ½ cup plant butter, room temperature
- 1 cup pure date sugar
- ½ cup oat milk
- 2 tsp vanilla extract
- 1 lemon, zested
- 1 cup dried raspberries

For the orange glaze:
- 2 tbsp orange juice
- 1 cup pure date sugar

Directions:
1. Preheat oven to 400°F and grease 6 muffin cups with cooking spray. In a small bowl, mix the flax seed powder with water and allow thickening for 5 minutes to make the flax egg. In a medium bowl, mix the flour, baking powder, and salt. In another bowl, cream the plant butter, date sugar, and flax egg. Mix in the oat milk, vanilla, and lemon zest.
2. Combine both mixtures, fold in raspberries, and fill muffin cups two-thirds way up with the batter. Bake until a toothpick inserted comes out clean, 20-25 minutes.
3. In a medium bowl, whisk orange juice and date sugar until smooth. Remove the muffins when ready and transfer them to a wire rack to cool. Drizzle the glaze on top to serve.

Nutrition:
- Calories 700
- Fats 25.5 g
- Carbs 115.1 g
- Protein 10.5 g

21. Berry Cream Compote Over Crepes

Preparation Time: 5-15 minutes
Cooking Time: 35 minutes
Servings: 4
Ingredients:
For the berry cream:
- 1 knob plant butter

- 2 tbsp pure date sugar
- 1 tsp vanilla extract
- ½ cup fresh blueberries
- ½ cup fresh raspberries
- ½ cup whipped coconut cream

For the crepes:
- 2 tbsp flax seed powder + 6 tbsp water
- 1 tsp vanilla extract
- 1 tsp pure date sugar
- ¼ tsp salt
- 2 cups almond flour
- 1 ½ cups almond milk
- 1 ½ cups water
- 3 tbsp plant butter for frying

Directions:
1. Melt butter in a pot over low heat and mix in the date sugar, and vanilla. Cook until the sugar melts and then, toss in berries. Allow softening for 2 to 3 minutes. Set aside to cool.
2. In a medium bowl, mix the flax seed powder with water and allow thickening for 5 minutes to make the flax egg. Whisk in the vanilla, date sugar, and salt.
3. Pour in a quarter cup of almond flour and whisk, then a quarter cup of almond milk, and mix until no lumps remain. Repeat the mixing process with the remaining almond flour and almond milk in the same quantities until exhausted.
4. Mix in 1 cup of water until the mixture is runny like that of pancakes, and add the remaining water until the mixture is lighter. Brush a large non-stick skillet with some butter and place over medium heat to melt.
5. Pour 1 tablespoon of the batter into the pan and swirl the skillet quickly and all around to coat the pan with the batter. Cook until the batter is dry and golden brown beneath, about 30 seconds.
6. Use a spatula to carefully flip the crepe and cook the other side until golden brown too. Fold the crepe onto a plate and set it aside. Repeat making more crepes with the remaining batter until exhausted. Plate the crepes, top with the whipped coconut cream and the berry compote. Serve immediately.

Nutrition:

- Calories 339
- Fats 24.5 g
- Carbs 30 g
- Protein 2.3 g

22. Irish Brown Bread

Preparation Time: 5-15 minutes
Cooking Time: 50 minutes
Servings: 4
Ingredients:
- 4 cups whole-wheat flour
- ¼ tsp salt
- ½ cup rolled oats
- 1 tsp baking soda
- 1 ¾ cups coconut milk, thick
- 2 tbsp pure maple syrup

Directions:
1. Preheat the oven to 400°F.
2. In a bowl, mix flour, salt, oats, and baking soda. Add in coconut milk, maple syrup and whisk until dough forms. Dust your hands with some flour and knead the dough into a ball. Shape the dough into a circle and place it on a baking sheet.
3. Cut a deep cross on the dough and bake in the oven for 15 minutes at 450°F. Then, reduce the temperature to 400°F and bake further for 20 to 25 minutes or until a hollow sound is made when the bottom of the bread is tapped. Slice and serve.

Nutrition:
- Calories 963
- Fats 44. g
- Carbs 125.1 g
- Protein 22.1 g

23. Mushroom Avocado Panini

Preparation Time: 5-15 minutes
Cooking Time: 30 minutes
Servings: 4
Ingredients:

- 1 tbsp olive oil
- 1 cup sliced white button mushrooms
- Salt and black pepper to taste
- 1 ripe avocado, pitted, peeled, and sliced
- 2 tbsp freshly squeezed lemon juice
- 1 tbsp chopped parsley
- ½ tsp pure maple syrup
- 8 slices whole-wheat ciabatta
- 4 oz sliced plant-based Parmesan cheese
- 1 tbsp olive oil

Directions:

1. Heat the olive oil in a medium skillet over medium heat and sauté the mushrooms until softened, 5 minutes. Season with salt and black pepper. Turn the heat off.
2. Preheat a panini press to medium heat, 3 to 5 minutes.
3. Mash the avocado in a medium bowl and mix in the lemon juice, parsley, and maple syrup.
4. Spread the mixture on 4 bread slices, divide the mushrooms and plant-based Parmesan cheese on top.
5. Cover with the other bread slices and brush the top with olive oil.
6. Grill the sandwiches one after another in the heated press until golden brown and the cheese melted.
7. Serve warm.

Nutrition:

- Calories 338
- Fats 22.4 g
- Carbs 25.5 g
- Protein 12.4 g

24.   Ricotta   Basil Pinwheels

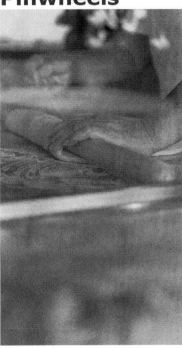

Preparation Time: 10 minutes
Cooking Time: 3-30 minutes
Servings: 4
Ingredients:

- ½ cup unsalted cashews
- Water
- 7 ounces firm tofu, cut into pieces
- ¼ cup almond milk
- 1 teaspoon white wine vinegar
- 1 clove garlic, smashed
- 20 to 25 fresh basil leaves
- Salt and pepper to taste
- 8 tortillas
- 7 ounces fresh spinach
- ½ cup black olives, sliced
- 2 to 3 tomatoes, cut into small pieces

Directions:
Soak the cashews for 30 minutes in enough water to cover them. Drain them well and pat them dry with paper towels. Place the cashews in a blender along with the tofu, almond milk, vinegar, garlic, basil leaves, salt, and pepper to taste. Blend until smooth and creamy. Spread the resulting mixture on the eight tortillas, dividing them equally. Top with spinach leaves, olives, and tomatoes. Tightly roll each loaded tortilla.

Cut off the ends with a sharp knife and slice into four or five pinwheels.

Nutrition:

- Calories 236
- Carbohydrates 6.1 g
- Fats 21.6 g
- Protein 4.2 g

25. Delicious Sloppy Joes With No Meat

Preparation Time: 6 minutes

Cooking Time: 5 minutes
Servings: 4
Ingredients:

- 5 tablespoons vegetable stock
- 2 stalks celery, diced
- 1 small onion, diced
- 1 small red bell pepper, diced
- 1 teaspoon garlic powder
- 1 teaspoon chili powder
- 1 teaspoon ground cumin
- 1 teaspoon salt
- 1 cup cooked bulgur wheat
- 1 cup red lentils
- 1 15-ounce can tomato sauce
- 4 tablespoons tomato paste
- 3½ cups water
- 2 teaspoons balsamic vinegar

- 1 tablespoon Hoisin sauce

Directions:

In a Dutch oven, heat the vegetable stock and add the celery, onion, and bell pepper. Sauté until vegetables are soft, about five minutes.

Add the garlic powder, chili powder, cumin, and salt and mix in.

Add the bulgur wheat, lentils, tomato sauce, tomato paste, water, vinegar, and Hoisin sauce. Stir and bring to a boil. Turn the heat down to a simmer and cook uncovered for 30 minutes. Stir occasionally to prevent sticking and scorching. Taste to see if the lentils are tender.

When the lentils are done, serve on buns.

Nutrition:

- Calories 451
- Fats 10 g
- Carbohydrates 61 g
- Protein 27 g

26. Garlic and White Bean Soup

Preparation Time: 10 minutes
Cooking Time: 10 minutes
Servings: 4
Ingredients:

- 45 ounces cooked cannellini beans
- 1/4 teaspoon dried thyme
- 2 teaspoons minced garlic
- 1/8 teaspoon crushed red pepper

- 1/2 teaspoon dried rosemary
- 1/8 teaspoon ground black pepper
- 2 tablespoons olive oil
- 4 cups vegetable broth

Directions:

Place one-third of white beans in a food processor, then pour in 2 cups broth and pulse for 2 minutes until smooth. Place a pot over medium heat, add oil and when hot, add garlic and cook for 1 minute until fragrant. Add pureed beans into the pan along with remaining beans, sprinkle with spices and herbs, pour in the broth, stir until combined, and bring the mixture to boil over medium-high heat. Switch heat to medium-low level, simmer the beans for 15 minutes, and then mash them with a fork. Taste the soup to adjust seasoning and then serve.

Nutrition:

- Calories: 222 Cal
- Fat: 7 g
- Carbs: 13 g
- Protein: 11.2 g
- Fiber: 9.1 g

27. Coconut Curry Lentils

Preparation Time: 10 minutes
Cooking Time: 40 minutes
Servings: 4
Ingredients:

- 1 cup brown lentils
- 1 small white onion, peeled, chopped
- 1 teaspoon minced garlic
- 1 teaspoon grated ginger
- 3 cups baby spinach
- 1 tablespoon curry powder
- 2 tablespoons olive oil

- 13 ounces coconut milk, unsweetened
- 2 cups vegetable broth

For Servings:
- 4 cups cooked rice
- 1/4 cup chopped cilantro

Directions:

Place a large pot over medium heat, add oil and when hot, add ginger and garlic and cook for 1 minute until fragrant. Add onion, cook for 5 minutes, stir in curry powder, cook for 1 minute until toasted, add lentils, and pour in broth. Switch heat to medium-high level, bring the mixture to a boil, then switch heat to the low level and simmer for 20 minutes until tender and all the liquid is absorbed. Pour in milk, stir until combined, turn heat to medium level, and simmer for 10 minutes until thickened. Then remove the pot from heat, stir in spinach, let it stand for 5 minutes until its leaves wilts and then top with cilantro.

Serve lentils with rice.

Nutrition:
- Calories: 184 Cal
- Fat: 3.7 g
- Carbs: 30 g
- Protein: 11.3 g
- Fiber: 10. 7 g

28. Black Bean Meatball Salad

Preparation Time: 10 minutes
Cooking Time: 25 minutes
Servings: 4

Ingredients:

For the Meatballs:
- 1/2 cup quinoa, cooked
- 1 cup cooked black beans
- 3 cloves of garlic, peeled
- 1 small red onion, peeled
- 1 teaspoon ground dried coriander
- 1 teaspoon ground dried cumin
- 1 teaspoon smoked paprika

For the Salad:
- 1 large sweet potato, peeled, diced
- 1 lemon, juiced
- 1 teaspoon minced garlic
- 1 cup coriander leaves
- 1/3 cup almonds
- 1/3 teaspoon ground black pepper
- ½ teaspoon salt
- 1 1/2 tablespoons olive oil

Directions:

Prepare the meatballs and for this, place beans and puree in a blender, pulse until pureed, and place this mixture in a medium bowl. Add onion and garlic, process until chopped, add to the bean mixture, add all the spices, stir until combined, and shape the mixture into uniform balls. Bake the balls on a greased baking sheet for 25 minutes at 350 degrees F until browned. Meanwhile, spread sweet potatoes on a baking sheet lined with baking paper, drizzle with ½ tablespoon oil, toss until coated, and bake for 20 minutes with the meatballs. Prepare the dressing, and for this, place remaining ingredients for the salad in a food processor and pulse until smooth. Place roasted sweet potatoes in a bowl, drizzle with the dressing, toss until coated, and then top with meatballs. Serve straight away.

Nutrition:
- Calories: 140 Cal
- Fat: 8 g
- Carbs: 8 g
- Protein: 10 g
- Fiber: 4 g

29.   Cauliflower-Onion Patties

Preparation Time: 05 minutes
Cooking Time: 10 minutes
Servings: 4
Ingredients:

- 3 cups cauliflower florets
- 1/2 cup onion
- 2 large eggs
- 2 tablespoons all-purpose white flour
- 2 tablespoons olive oil

Directions:
Dice cauliflower and chop onion. Boil the diced cauliflower in a small amount of water for 5 minutes; drain. Break eggs into a medium bowl and beat. Add the flour and mix well. Add the cauliflower and onion and stir into the flour/egg mixture until well mixed. Add olive oil to a frying pan and heat. Drop the mixture by spoonful's into the hot oil, making 4 equal portions (or 8 portions in a smaller size are desired).
Using a spatula, flatten the latkes and fry until brown on both sides.
Drain on a paper towel to soak up extra oil. Serve hot.

Nutrition:

- Calories 134
- Total Fat 9.6g
- Saturated Fat 1.8g
- Cholesterol 93mg
- Sodium 58mg
- Total Carbohydrate 8.5g
- Dietary Fiber 2.3g
- Total Sugars 2.6g
- Protein 5.2g
- Calcium 34mg
- Iron 1mg
- Potassium 286mg
- Phosphorus 229 mg

30. Roasted Garlic Broccoli

Preparation Time: 15 minutes
Cooking Time: 25 minutes
Servings: 4
Ingredients:

- 2 tablespoons minced garlic
- 3 tablespoons olive oil
- 1 large head of broccoli, separated into florets
- 1/3 cup grated Parmesan cheese
- Salt and black pepper to taste
- 1 tablespoon chopped fresh basil

Directions:
Preheat the oven to 450 degrees F. Grease a large casserole dish.

Place the olive oil and garlic in a large resealable bag. Add broccoli, and shake to mix. Pour into the prepared casserole dish, and season with salt and pepper to taste. Bake for 25 minutes, stirring halfway through. Top with Parmesan cheese and basil, and broil for 3 to 5 minutes, until golden brown.

Nutrition:
- Calories 112
- Total Fat 11.1g
- Saturated Fat 1.8g
- Cholesterol 2mg
- Sodium 30mg
- Total Carbohydrate 3g
- Dietary Fiber 0.7g
- Total Sugars 0.4g
- Protein 1.7g
- Calcium 40mg
- Iron 0mg
- Potassium 91mg
- Phosphorus 89 mg

31. Carrot Casserole

Preparation Time: 15 minutes
Cooking Time: 15 minutes
Servings: 4
Ingredients:
- ½ pound carrots
- ½ cup graham crackers
- 1 tablespoon olive oil
- 1 tablespoon onion
- 1/8 teaspoon black pepper
- 1/6 cup shredded cheddar cheese

- Salt

Directions:
Preheat oven to 350º F. Peel carrots and slice them into 1/4-inch rounds. Place carrots in a large saucepan over medium-high heat and boil until soft enough to mash. Drain and reserve 1/3-cup liquid. Mash carrots until they are smooth. Crush graham crackers, heat oil, and minced onion. Stir crackers, onion, oil, salt, pepper, and reserved liquid into mashed carrots. Place in a greased small casserole dish. Sprinkle shredded cheese on top and bake for 15 minutes. Serve hot.

Nutrition:
- Calories 118
- Total Fat 6.1g
- Saturated Fat 1.7g
- Cholesterol 5mg
- Sodium 86mg
- Total Carbohydrate 14g
- Dietary Fiber 1.8g
- Total Sugars 6.2g
- Protein 2.4g
- Calcium 56mg
- Iron 1mg
- Potassium 205mg
- Phosphorus 189 mg

32. Carrot-Pineapple Casserole

Preparation Time: 10 minutes
Cooking Time: 50 minutes
Servings: 4

Ingredients:
- 3 large carrots
- 1 large pineapple
- 2 tablespoons all-purpose flour
- 1 tablespoon honey
- ½ teaspoon ground cinnamon
- 1 tablespoon olive oil
- 1/2 cup pineapple juice

Directions:
Preheat oven to 350 degrees F. Peel and slice carrots and pineapples. Bring 1 quart of water to a boil in a medium-sized pot. Boil carrots for 5 minutes or until tender. Drain. Layer carrots and pineapples in a large casserole dish. Using a fork, mix flour, honey, and cinnamon in a small bowl. Mix in olive oil to make a crumb topping. Sprinkle flour mixture over carrots and pineapples then drizzle with juice. Bake for 50 minutes or until pineapples and carrots are tender and the topping is golden brown.

Nutrition:
- Calories 94
- Total Fat 2.9g
- Saturated Fat 0.4g
- Cholesterol 0mg
- Sodium 31mg
- Total Carbohydrate 17.4g
- Dietary Fiber 1.8g
- Total Sugars 11.2g
- Protein 0.9g
- Calcium 23mg
- Iron 0mg
- Potassium 206mg
- Phosphorus 27 mg

33. Grilled Summer Squash

Preparation Time: 05 minutes
Cooking Time: 10 minutes
Servings: 4
Ingredients:
- 2 medium summer squash
- Non-stick cooking spray
- 1/4 teaspoon garlic powder
- 1/4 teaspoon black pepper

Directions:
Wash summer squash with mild soap and water; rinse well.
Cut each squash into four pieces; cut both vertically and horizontally.
Place on a cookie sheet or large platter and spray with non-stick cooking spray. Sprinkle with garlic powder and black pepper, to taste (both optional). Cook on either a gas grill. Cook for approximately three to five minutes, flipping once. The squash should be tender but not mushy. If cooking on a gas grill, place a flat surface down on a sheet of aluminum foil sprayed with non-stick cooking spray.
approximately 2 more minutes on the "round" side.

Nutrition:
- Calories 17
- Total Fat 0.2g
- Saturated Fat 0.1g
- Cholesterol 0mg
- Sodium 2mg
- Total Carbohydrate 3.4g
- Dietary Fiber 0.9g
- Total Sugars 3g
- Protein 0.9g
- Calcium 18mg
- Iron 0mg

- Potassium 190mg
- Phosphorus100mg

34. Pineapple and Pepper Curry

Preparation Time: 5 minutes
Cooking Time: 15 minutes
Servings: 4
Ingredients:
- 2 cups green bell pepper
- 1/2 cup red onion
- 1 tablespoon cilantro
- 1 tablespoon ginger root
- 2 tablespoons olive oil
- 1/2 cup pineapple juice
- 1 teaspoon curry powder
- 1/2 tablespoon lemon juice

Directions:
Chop bell pepper, onion, and cilantro. Shred ginger root.
Heat oil and when hot add ginger and red onion. Cook until the onion is transparent. Microwave peppers on high for 6 minutes. Add the peppers to the onion mixture. Close the lid of the pan and cook on low for 10 minutes, stirring to avoid burning peppers. Add pineapple juice and simmer for 2 minutes. Add curry powder and cilantro. Turn the vegetables once and let simmer on low for 2 minutes. Garnish lemon juice before serving.
Nutrition:
- Calories 107
- Total Fat 6g
- Saturated Fat 0.8g
- Cholesterol 0mg
- Sodium 4mg

- Total Carbohydrate 12.5g
- Dietary Fiber 2.6g
- Total Sugars 7.1g
- Protein 2.3g
- Calcium 20mg
- Iron 1mg
- Potassium 222mg
- Phosphorus150mg

35. Stuffed Mushrooms

Preparation Time: 25 minutes
Cooking Time: 20 minutes
Servings: 4
Ingredients:
- 8 whole fresh mushrooms
- ½ tablespoon olive oil
- ½ tablespoon minced garlic
- 1 (8-ounce package cream cheese, softened
- 1/8 cup grated Parmesan cheese
- 1/8 teaspoon ground black pepper
- 1/8 teaspoon onion powder
- 1/8 teaspoon ground cayenne pepper

Directions:
Preheat oven to 350 degrees F. Sprays a baking sheet with cooking spray. Clean mushrooms with a damp paper towel. Carefully break off stems. Chop stems extremely fine, discarding tough end of stems.
Heat oil in a large skillet over medium heat. Add garlic and chopped mushroom stems to the skillet. Fry until any moisture has disappeared, taking care not to burn the garlic. Set aside to cool. When the garlic and mushroom mixture is no longer hot, stir in

cream cheese, Parmesan cheese, black pepper, onion powder, and cayenne pepper. The mixture should be very thick. Using a little spoon, fill each mushroom cap with a generous amount of stuffing. Arrange the mushroom caps on the prepared cookie sheet. Bake for 20 minutes in the preheated oven, or until the mushrooms are piping hot and liquid starts to form under caps.

Nutrition:
- Calories 150
- Total Fat 14.5g
- Saturated Fat 8.6g
- Cholesterol 42mg
- Sodium 171mg
- Total Carbohydrate 2g
- Dietary Fiber 0.4g
- Total Sugars 0.3g
- Protein 3.6g
- Calcium 37mg
- Iron 1mg
- Potassium 50mg
- Phosphorus 10mg

36. Sautéed Mushrooms

Preparation Time: 10 minutes
Cooking Time: 15 minutes
Servings: 4
Ingredients:
- 3 tablespoons olive oil
- 3 tablespoons unsalted butter
- 1 pound button mushrooms, sliced
- 1 clove garlic, thinly sliced
- 1/8 teaspoon salt, or to taste
- Freshly ground black pepper to taste

Directions:
Heat olive oil and unsalted butter in a large saucepan over medium heat. Cook and stir mushrooms, garlic, salt, and black pepper in the hot oil and butter until mushrooms are lightly browned, about 5 minutes. Reduce heat to low and simmer until mushrooms are tender, 5 to 8 more minutes.

Nutrition:
- Calories 171
- Total Fat 19.2g
- Saturated Fat 7g
- Cholesterol 23mg
- Sodium 62mg
- Total Carbohydrate 0.9g
- Dietary Fiber 0.2g
- Total Sugars 0.3g
- Protein 0.7g
- Calcium 4mg
- Iron 1mg
- Potassium 62mg
- Phosphorus 50mg

37. Zucchini Stir-Fry

Preparation Time: 10 minutes
Cooking Time: 5 minutes
Servings: 4
Ingredients:
- 1 tablespoon olive oil
- 1 teaspoon cumin
- 2 cups zucchini
- 1/2 cup red onion

- 1 teaspoon black pepper
- 1 tablespoon lemon juice
- 1/4 cup fresh parsley

Directions:

Peel and slice zucchini and onion. Chop parsley. Heat olive oil in a non-stick skillet over medium heat.

Sauté cumin to brown. Add zucchini and onion and sprinkle with black pepper. Stir a few times to mix. Cover and cook for approximately 5 minutes to medium tenderness, stirring a few times. Add lemon juice and chopped parsley. Mix, cook another minute, and serve.

Nutrition:

- Calories 51
- Total Fat 3.8g
- Saturated Fat 0.6g
- Cholesterol 0mg
- Sodium 11mg
- Total Carbohydrate 4.3g
- Dietary Fiber 1.3g
- Total Sugars 1.8g
- Protein 1.2g
- Calcium 25mg
- Iron 1mg
- Potassium 225mg
- Phosphorus 108mg

38. Couscous Primavera

Preparation Time: 15 minutes
Cooking Time: 20 minutes

Servings: 4

Ingredients:

- 1 cup dry couscous
- ½ cup broccoli
- 1/2 cup chopped green onions
- 2 tablespoons olive oil
- 1/2 teaspoon ground cumin
- 1 pinch ground black pepper
- 2 cups water
- 1 bunch asparagus, trimmed and cut into 1/4-inch pieces
- 1 cup shelled fresh or thawed frozen beans
- 2 tablespoons chopped fresh basil
- Salt and freshly ground black pepper to taste

Directions:

Combine couscous, green onion, broccoli, olive oil, cumin, and black pepper in a large bowl; stir until the olive oil is completely incorporated. Bring water, asparagus, and beans to a boil in a saucepan over high heat. Pour water, asparagus, and peas over the couscous mixture; shake the bowl to settle couscous into liquid. Cover and let stand for 10 minutes. Fluff with a fork, then stir in basil and season with salt and pepper to taste.

Nutrition:

- Calories 174
- Total Fat 5g
- Saturated Fat 0.7g
- Cholesterol 0mg
- Sodium 57mg
- Total Carbohydrate 26.9g
- Dietary Fiber 3.2g
- Total Sugars 1.6g
- Protein 5.6g
- Calcium 24mg
- Iron 1mg
- Potassium 124mg
- Phosphorus 108mg

39. Lemon Pepper Beans

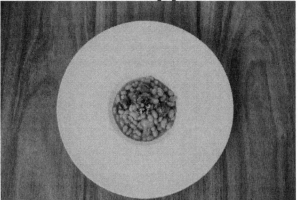

Preparation Time: 01 minutes
Cooking Time: 5 minutes
Servings: 4
Ingredients:

- 1 cup frozen green beans, thawed
- 1 tablespoon water
- 2 tablespoons olive oil
- 1 pinch lemon pepper
- 1 pinch dried rosemary

Directions:
Place the beans and water into a microwave-safe bowl. Cover loosely, and microwave for 3 to 4 minutes, or until beans are tender. Stir in oil, and sprinkle with lemon pepper and rosemary. Serve warm.

Nutrition:

- Calories 90
- Total Fat 7.2g
- Saturated Fat 1g
- Cholesterol 0mg
- Sodium 2mg
- Total Carbohydrate 5.3g
- Dietary Fiber 1.9g
- Total Sugars 2.1g
- Protein 2g
- Calcium 10mg
- Iron 1mg
- Potassium 89mg
- Phosphorus 45 mg

40. Mushroom Rice

Preparation Time: 5 minutes
Cooking Time: 25 minutes
Servings: 4
Ingredients:

- 2 teaspoons olive oil
- 6 mushrooms, coarsely chopped
- 1 clove garlic, minced
- 1 green onion, finely chopped
- 1 cup uncooked white rice
- 1/2 teaspoon chopped fresh parsley
- Salt and pepper to taste
- 1-1/2 cups water

Directions:
Heat olive oil in a saucepan over medium heat. Cook mushrooms, garlic, and green onion until mushrooms are cooked and liquid has evaporated. Stir in water and rice. Season with parsley, salt, and pepper. Reduce heat, cover, and simmer for 20 minutes.

Nutrition:

- Calories 197
- Total Fat 2.7g
- Saturated Fat 0.4g
- Cholesterol 0mg
- Sodium 5mg
- Total Carbohydrate 38.4g
- Dietary Fiber 1g
- Total Sugars 0.6g
- Protein 4.3g
- Calcium 17mg
- Iron 3mg
- Potassium 154mg
- Phosphorus 110mg

41. Broccoli with Garlic Butter and Almonds

Preparation Time: 10 minutes
Cooking Time: 50 minutes
Servings: 4
Ingredients:
- 1 pound fresh broccoli, cut into bite-size pieces
- ¼ cup olive oil
- ½ tablespoon honey
- 1-1/2 tablespoons soy sauce
- ¼ teaspoon ground black pepper
- 2 cloves garlic, minced
- ¼ cup chopped almonds

Directions:
Place the broccoli into a large pot with about 1 inch of water in the bottom. Bring to a boil, and cook for 7 minutes, or until tender but still crisp. Drain, and arrange broccoli on a serving platter. While the broccoli is cooking, heat the oil in a small skillet over medium heat. Mix in the honey, soy sauce, pepper, and garlic. Bring to a boil, then remove from the heat. Mix in the almonds, and pour the sauce over the broccoli. Serve immediately.

Nutrition:
- Calories 177
- Total Fat 17.3g
- Saturated Fat 2.1g
- Cholesterol 0mg
- Sodium 234mg
- Total Carbohydrate 5.3g
- Dietary Fiber 1.2g
- Total Sugars 2.7g
- Protein 2.9g
- Calcium 20mg
- Iron 1mg
- Potassium 131mg
- Phosphorus 67 mg

42. Roasted Vegetables

Preparation Time: 15 minutes
Cooking Time: 40 minutes
Servings: 4
Ingredients:
- ¼ summer squash, cubed
- 1 red bell peppers, seeded and diced
- 1 red onion, quartered
- ¼ cup green beans
- 1 tablespoon chopped fresh thyme
- 2 tablespoons chopped fresh rosemary
- 1/4 cup olive oil
- ½ tablespoon lemon juice
- Salt and freshly ground black pepper

Directions:
Preheat oven to 475 degrees F. In a large bowl, combine the squash, red bell peppers, and green beans. Separate the red onion quarters into pieces, and add them to the mixture. In a small bowl, stir

together thyme, rosemary, olive oil, lemon juice, salt, and pepper. Toss with vegetables until they are coated. Spread evenly on a large roasting pan. Roast for 35 to 40 minutes in the preheated oven, stirring every 10 minutes, or until vegetables are cooked through and browned.

Nutrition:
- Calories 145
- Total Fat 13.1g
- Saturated Fat 2g
- Cholesterol 0mg
- Sodium 4mg
- Total Carbohydrate 8g
- Dietary Fiber 2.5g
- Total Sugars 3.5g
- Protein 1.3g
- Calcium 47mg
- Iron 2mg
- Potassium 160mg
- Phosphorus 110mg

43. Honey Roasted Cauliflower

Preparation Time: 10 minutes
Cooking Time: 35 minutes
Servings: 4

Ingredients:
- 2 cups cauliflower
- 2 tablespoons diced onion
- 2 tablespoons olive oil
- 1 tablespoon honey
- 1 teaspoon dry mustard
- 1 pinch salt
- 1 pinch ground black pepper

Directions:
Preheat oven to 375 degrees F. Lightly coats an 11x7 inch baking dish with non-stick cooking spray. Place cauliflower in a single layer in prepared dish, and top with onion. In a small bowl, combine olive oil, honey, mustard, salt, and pepper; drizzle over cauliflower and onion.

Bake in the preheated 375 degrees F oven for 35 minutes or until tender, stirring halfway through the cooking time.

Nutrition:
- Calories 88
- Total Fat 7.3g
- Saturated Fat 1g
- Cholesterol 0mg
- Sodium 47mg
- Total Carbohydrate 6.4g
- Dietary Fiber 0.9g
- Total Sugars 5.2g
- Protein 0.8g
- Calcium 11mg
- Iron 0mg
- Potassium 92mg
- Phosphorus 70mg

44. Okra Curry

Preparation Time: 5 minutes
Cooking Time: 10 minutes
Servings: 4

Ingredients:

- 1 pound okra, ends trimmed, cut into 1/4-inch rounds
- 1 tablespoon olive oil
- 1/2 teaspoon curry powder
- 1/2 teaspoon all-purpose flour
- 1/2 teaspoon black pepper

Directions:

Microwave the okra on High for 3 minutes. Heat olive oil in a large skillet over medium heat. Gently mix in the curry powder, all-purpose flour, and black pepper; cook 2 minutes more. Serve immediately.

Nutrition:

- Calories 45
- Total Fat 3.7g
- Saturated Fat 0.5g
- Cholesterol 0mg
- Sodium 3mg
- Total Carbohydrate 2.7g
- Dietary Fiber 1g
- Total Sugars 0.4g
- Protein 0.7g
- Calcium 28mg
- Iron 1mg
- Potassium 92mg
- Phosphorus 60 mg

45. Cranberry Cabbage

Preparation Time: 10 minutes
Cooking Time: 15 minutes
Servings: 4

Ingredients:

- 8 ounces canned whole-berry cranberry sauce
- 1 tablespoon fresh lemon juice
- 1/4 teaspoon ground cloves
- 1 medium head red cabbage

Directions:

In a large pan heat cranberry sauce, lemon juice, and cloves together and bring to a simmer. Stir cabbage into melted cranberry sauce, mixing well. Bring mixture to a boil; reduce heat to simmer. Continue cooking until cabbage is tender, stirring occasionally. Serve hot.

Nutrition:

- Calories 38
- Total Fat 0.1g
- Saturated Fat 0g
- Cholesterol 0mg
- Sodium 20mg
- Total Carbohydrate 7.9g
- Dietary Fiber 2.6g
- Total Sugars 3.8g
- Protein 1g
- Calcium 37mg
- Iron 1mg
- Potassium 224mg
- Phosphorus 120 mg
-

46. Bean, Eggs, and Avocado

Preparation Time: 5 minutes
Cooking Time: 5 minutes
Servings: 2
Ingredients:

- 2 tsp rapeseed oil
- 1 red chilli, deseeded and thinly sliced
- 1 large garlic clove, sliced
- 2 large eggs
- 400g can black beans
- ½ x 400g can cherry tomatoes
- ¼ tsp cumin seeds
- 1 small avocado, halved and sliced
- handful fresh, chopped coriander
- 1 lime, cut into wedges

Directions:

In a big nonstick frying pan, heat the oil. Cook until the chili and garlic have softened and begun to color. On both sides of the plate, crack the eggs. Spoon the beans (with their juice) and tomatoes around the pan until they've started to set, then scatter the cumin seeds on top. Instead of cooking the beans and tomatoes, you want to steam them up. Remove the pan from the heat and add the avocado and coriander to the top. Half of the lime wedges should be squeezed over the top. The leftover wedges should be served on the side for squeezing over.

Nutrition per serving:

- Kcal: 356
- Fat: 20g
- Saturates: 4g
- Carbs: 18g
- Sugars: 5g
- Fibre: 11g
- Protein: 20g
- Salt: 0.8g

47. Omelet with Tomatoes Fried

Preparation Time: 5 minutes
Cooking Time: 5 minutes
Servings: 2
Ingredients:

- 1 tsp rapeseed oil
- 3 tomatoes , halved
- 4 large eggs
- 1 tbsp chopped parsley
- 1 tbsp chopped basil

Directions:

In a small nonstick frying pan, heat the oil and cook the tomatoes cut-side down until they begin to soften and color. In a shallow cup, whisk together the eggs, spices, and plenty of freshly ground black pepper. Scoop the tomatoes out of the pan and divide them into two bowls. Pour the egg mixture into the pan and stir gently with a wooden spoon to allow the uncooked egg to flow into the gap created by the egg that has set on the pan's bottom. When it's almost over, stop stirring and let it set into an omelet. Serve with the tomatoes, cut into four halves.

Nutrition per serving:

- Kcal: 204
- Fat: 13g
- Saturates: 3g
- Carbs: 4g
- Sugars: 4g
- Fibre: 1g
- Protein: 17g
- Salt: 0.5g

Chapter 3. Dinner

48. Stir-Fry Vegetables

Preparation Time: 10 minutes
Cooking Time: 20 minutes
Servings: 4
Ingredients:

- 2 cups green pepper
- 2 cups red pepper
- 1 cup fresh sliced mushrooms
- 1 cup celery
- ¼ cup onion
- 1 garlic clove
- ½ teaspoon honey
- ½ teaspoon dried oregano
- 1/8 teaspoon salt
- 1/8 teaspoon pepper
- 1 tablespoon olive oil

Directions:
Cut green and red peppers. Slice celery and chop onion. Crush garlic.
In a large skillet, heat oil. Add green pepper, red pepper, mushrooms, celery, onion, garlic, honey, oregano, salt, and pepper. Stir-fry over medium-high heat until peppers are crisp-tender. Serve hot.

Nutrition:

- Calories 36
- Total Fat 1.6g
- Saturated Fat 0.2g
- Cholesterol 0mg
- Sodium 69mg
- Total Carbohydrate 5.4g
- Dietary Fiber 1.2g
- Total Sugars 2.6g
- Protein 0.9g
- Calcium 13mg
- Iron 1mg
- Potassium 162mg
- Phosphorus 120mg

49. Roasted Apples and Cabbage

Preparation Time: 15 minutes
Cooking Time: 20 minutes
Servings: 4
Ingredients:

- 1 cup chopped cabbage
- 2 apples - peeled, cored, and cut into 3/4-inch chunks
- 2 tablespoons olive oil, or as needed
- Salt and ground black pepper to taste
- 1 pinch garlic powder to taste
- Zest from 1 lemon
- Juice from 1 lemon

Directions:
Preheat oven to 425 degrees F. Arrange cabbage in a single layer on a rimmed baking sheet; sprinkle apple pieces evenly around the baking sheet. Drizzle the cabbage, apples with olive oil; sprinkle with salt, black pepper, and garlic powder. Toss the mixture gently to coat.
Roast in the preheated oven until cabbage is hot and fragrant, about 20 minutes. Sprinkle with lemon zest, and squeeze juice from zested lemon over the cabbage to serve.

Nutrition:

- Calories 127
- Total Fat 7.3g
- Saturated Fat 1g
- Cholesterol 0mg
- Sodium 4mg
- Total Carbohydrate 17.8g
- Dietary Fiber 3.6g
- Total Sugars 12.5g
- Protein 0.7g
- Calcium 11mg
- Iron 1mg
- Potassium 170mg
- Phosphorus 80mg

50. Cabbage Bake

Preparation Time: 15 minutes
Cooking Time: 30 minutes
Servings: 4
Ingredients:
- 1 cup water
- 1 cup cabbage
- ½ tablespoon olive oil
- 1 egg, beaten
- ½ cup shredded Cheddar cheese
- ½ cup graham crackers

Directions:
Preheat oven to 350 degrees F. Bring water to a boil in a medium saucepan. Place chopped cabbage in the water, and return to boil. Reduce heat, and simmer 2 minutes, until tender; drain. In a medium bowl, mix cabbage with oil, egg, Cheddar cheese, and 1/3 cup graham crackers. Transfer to a medium baking dish and top with remaining graham crackers. Cover, and bake 25 minutes in the preheated oven, until bubbly. Uncover, and continue baking for 5 minutes, until lightly browned.

Nutrition:
- Calories 91
- Total Fat 5.7g
- Saturated Fat 2.5g
- Cholesterol 37mg
- Sodium 114mg
- Total Carbohydrate 6.2g
- Dietary Fiber 0.5g
- Total Sugars 2.7g
- Protein 3.9g

- Calcium 79mg
- Iron 1mg
- Potassium 49mg
- Phosphorus 20mg

51. Grilled Tempeh with Green Beans

Preparation Time: 15-30 minutes
Cooking Time: 15 minutes
Servings: 4
Ingredients:
- 1 tbsp plant butter, melted
- 1 lb tempeh, sliced into 4 pieces
- 1 lb green beans, trimmed
- Salt and black pepper to taste
- 2 sprigs thyme
- 2 tbsp olive oil
- 1 tbsp pure corn syrup
- 1 lemon, juiced

Directions:
1. Preheat a grill pan over medium heat and brush with the plant butter.
2. Season the tempeh and green beans with salt, black pepper, and place the thyme in the pan. Grill the tempeh and green beans on both sides until golden brown and tender, 10 minutes.
3. Transfer to serving plates.
4. In a small bowl, whisk the olive oil, corn syrup, lemon juice, and drizzle all over the food.
5. Serve warm.

Nutrition:
- Calories 352
- Fats 22.5 g
- Carbs 21.8 g
- Protein 22.6 g

52. Creamy Fettucine with Peas

Preparation Time: 15-30 minutes
Cooking Time: 25 minutes
Servings: 4
Ingredients:

- 16 oz whole-wheat fettuccine
- Salt and black pepper to taste
- ¾ cup flax milk
- ½ cup cashew butter, room temperature
- 1 tbsp olive oil
- 2 garlic cloves, minced
- 1 ½ cups frozen peas
- ½ cup chopped fresh basil

Directions:

1. Add the fettuccine and 10 cups of water to a large pot, and cook over medium heat until al dente, 10 minutes. Drain the pasta through a colander and set it aside. In a bowl, whisk the flax milk, cashew butter, and salt until smooth. Set aside.
2. Heat the olive oil in a large skillet and sauté the garlic until fragrant, 30 seconds. Mix in the peas, fettuccine, and basil. Toss well until the pasta is well-coated in the sauce and season with some black pepper. Dish the food and serve warm.

Nutrition:

- Calories 654
- Fats 23.7 g
- Carbs 101.9 g
- Protein 18.2 g

53. Buckwheat Cabbage Rolls

Preparation Time: 15-30 minutes
Cooking Time: 30 minutes
Servings: 4
Ingredients:

- 2 tbsp plant butter
- 2 cups extra-firm tofu, pressed and crumbled
- ½ medium sweet onion, finely chopped
- 2 garlic cloves, minced
- Salt and black pepper to taste
- 1 cup buckwheat groats
- 1 ¾ cups vegetable stock
- 1 bay leaf
- 2 tbsp chopped fresh cilantro + more for garnishing
- 1 head Savoy cabbage, leaves separated (scraps kept)
- 1 (23 oz) canned chopped tomatoes

Directions:

1. Melt the plant butter in a large bowl and cook the tofu until golden brown, 8 minutes. Stir in the onion and garlic until softened and fragrant, 3 minutes. Season with salt, black pepper and mix in the buckwheat, bay leaf, and vegetable stock.

2. Close the lid, allow boiling, and then simmer until all the liquid is absorbed. Open the lid; remove the bay leaf, adjust the taste with salt, black pepper, and mix in the cilantro.
3. Lay the cabbage leaves on a flat surface and add 3 to 4 tablespoons of the cooked buckwheat onto each leaf. Roll the leaves to secure the filling firmly.
4. Pour the tomatoes with juices into a medium pot, season with a little salt, black pepper, and lay the cabbage rolls in the sauce. Cook over medium heat until the cabbage softens, 5 to 8 minutes. Turn the heat off and dish the food onto serving plates. Garnish with more cilantro and serve warm.

Nutrition:
- Calories 1147
- Fats 112.9 g
- Carbs 25.6 g
- Protein 23.8 g

54. Bbq Black Bean Burgers

Preparation Time: 15-30 minutes
Cooking Time: 20 minutes
Servings: 4
Ingredients:
- 3 (15 oz) cans black beans, drained and rinsed
- 2 tbsp whole-wheat flour
- 2 tbsp quick-cooking oats
- ¼ cup chopped fresh basil
- 2 tbsp pure barbecue sauce

- 1 garlic clove, minced
- Salt and black pepper to taste
- 4 whole-grain hamburger buns, split

For topping:
- Red onion slices
- Tomato slices
- Fresh basil leaves
- Additional barbecue sauce

Directions:
1. In a medium bowl, mash the black beans and mix in the flour, oats, basil, barbecue sauce, garlic salt, and black pepper until well combined. Mold 4 patties out of the mixture and set aside.
2. Heat a grill pan to medium heat and lightly grease with cooking spray.
3. Cook the bean patties on both sides until light brown and cooked through, 10 minutes.
4. Place the patties between the burger buns and top with the onions, tomatoes, basil, and some barbecue sauce.
5. Serve warm.

Nutrition:
- Calories 589
- Fats 17.7 g
- Carbs 80.9 g
- Protein 27.9 g

55. Paprika & Tomato Pasta Primavera

Preparation Time: 15-30 minutes
Cooking Time: 25 minutes
Servings: 4
Ingredients:
- 2 tbsp olive oil
- 8 oz whole-wheat fidelini
- ½ tsp paprika
- 1 small red onion, sliced
- 2 garlic cloves, minced
- 1 cup dry white wine
- Salt and black pepper to taste
- 2 cups cherry tomatoes, halved
- 3 tbsp plant butter, cut into ½-in cubes
- 1 lemon, zested and juiced
- 1 cup packed fresh basil leaves

Directions:
1. Heat the olive oil in a large pot and mix in the fidelini, paprika, onion, garlic, and stir-fry for 2-3 minutes.
2. Mix in the white wine, salt, and black pepper. Cover with water. Cook until the water absorbs and the fidelini al dente, 5 minutes. Mix in the cherry tomatoes, plant butter, lemon zest, lemon juice, and basil leaves.
3. Dish the food and serve warm.

Nutrition:
- Calories 380
- Fats 24.1 g
- Carbs 33.7 g
- Protein 11.2 g

56. Zucchini Rolls In Tomato Sauce

Preparation Time: 15-30 minutes
Cooking Time: 60 minutes
Servings: 4
Ingredients:
- 3 large zucchinis, sliced lengthwise into strips
- Salt and black pepper to taste
- 1 tbsp olive oil
- ¾ lb crumbled tempeh
- 1 cup crumbled tofu cheese
- 1/3 cup grated plant-based Parmesan cheese
- ¼ cup chopped fresh basil leaves
- 2 garlic cloves, minced
- 1 ½ cups marinara sauce, divided
- 2 cups shredded plant-based mozzarella, divided

Directions:
1. Line a baking sheet with paper towels and lay the zucchini slices in a single layer on the sheet. Sprinkle each side with some salt and allow releasing of liquid for 15 minutes.
2. Heat the olive oil in a large skillet over medium heat and cook the tempeh until browned, 10 minutes. Set aside.
3. In a medium bowl, mix the tempeh, tofu cheese, plant Parmesan cheese, basil and garlic; season with salt and black pepper.
4. Preheat the oven to 400°F.
5. Spread 1 cup of marinara sauce onto the bottom of a 10-inch oven-proof skillet and set aside.
6. Spread 1 tbsp of the cheese mixture evenly along with each zucchini slice; sprinkle with 1 tbsp of plant mozzarella cheese. Roll up the zucchini slices over the filling and arrange them in the skillet. Top with the remaining ½ cup of marinara sauce and sprinkle with the remaining plant mozzarella.
7. Bake in the oven for 25-30 minutes or until the zucchini rolls are heated through and the cheese begins to brown. Serve immediately.

Nutrition:
- Calories 428
- Fats 14.5 g
- Carbs 31.3 g
- Protein 40.3 g

57. Cannellini Beans Bow Ties

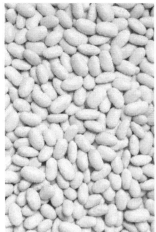

Preparation Time: 15-30 minutes
Cooking Time: 35 minutes
Servings: 4
Ingredients:
- 2 ½ cups whole-wheat bow tie pasta
- 1 tbsp olive oil
- 1 medium zucchini, sliced
- 2 garlic cloves, minced
- 2 large tomatoes, chopped
- 1 (15 oz) can cannellini beans, rinsed and drained
- 1 (2 ¼ oz) can pitted green olives, sliced
- ½ cup crumbled tofu cheese

Directions:
1. Cook the pasta in 8 cups of slightly salted water in a medium pot over medium heat until al dente, 10 minutes. Drain the pasta and set it aside.
2. Heat olive oil in a skillet and sauté zucchini and garlic for 4 minutes. Stir in tomatoes, beans, and olives. Cook until the tomatoes soften, 10 minutes. Mix in pasta. Allow warming for 1 minute. Stir in tofu cheese and serve warm.

Nutrition:
- Calories 206
- Fats 5.1 g
- Carbs 35.8 g
- Protein 7.6 g

58. White Bean Stuffed Squash

Preparation Time: 15-30 minutes
Cooking Time: 60 minutes
Servings: 4
Ingredients:
- 2 pounds large acorn squash
- 2 tbsp olive oil
- 3 garlic cloves, minced
- 1 (15 oz) can white beans, drained and rinsed
- 1 cup chopped spinach leaves
- ½ cup vegetable stock
- Salt and black pepper to taste
- ½ tsp cumin powder
- ½ tsp chili powder

Directions:
1. Preheat the oven to 350°F.
2. Cut the squash in half and scoop out the seeds.
3. Season with salt and pepper and place face down on a sheet pan. Bake for 45 minutes.
4. While the squash cooks, heat the olive oil in a medium pot over medium heat.
5. Sauté the garlic until fragrant, 30 seconds and mix in the beans. Cook for 1 minute.
6. Stir in the spinach, allow wilting for 2 minutes and season with salt, black pepper, cumin powder, and chili powder. Cook for 2 minutes and turn the heat off.
7. When the squash is fork-tender, remove it from the oven and fill the holes with the bean and spinach mixture.
8. Serve warm.

Nutrition:
- Calories 365
- Fats 34.6 g
- Carbs 16.7 g
- Protein 2.3 g

59. Grilled Zucchini and Spinach Pizza

Preparation Time: 15-30 minutes
Cooking Time: 30 minutes
Servings: 4
Ingredients:
For the pizza crust:
- 3 ½ cups whole-wheat flour
- 1 tsp yeast
- 1 tsp salt
- 1 pinch sugar
- 3 tbsp olive oil
- 1 cup warm water

For the topping:
- 1 cup marinara sauce
- 2 large zucchinis, sliced
- ½ cup chopped spinach
- ¼ cup pitted and sliced black olives
- ½ cup grated plant Parmesan cheese

Directions:
1. Preheat the oven the 350°F and lightly grease a pizza pan with cooking spray.
2. In a medium bowl, mix the flour, nutritional yeast, salt, sugar, olive oil, and warm water until smooth dough forms. Allow rising for an hour or until the dough doubles in size. Spread the dough on the pizza pan and apply the pizza sauce on top.
3. Meanwhile, heat a grill pan over medium heat, season the zucchinis with salt, black pepper, and cook in the pan until slightly charred on both sides.
4. Sit the cucumbers on the pizza crust and top with the spinach, olives, and plant Parmesan

cheese. Bake the pizza for 20 minutes or until the cheese melts. Remove from the oven, cool for 5 minutes, slice, and serve.

Nutrition:
- Calories 519
- Fats 13.4 g
- Carbs 87.5 g
- Protein 19.6 g

60. Crispy Tofu Burgers

Preparation Time: 15-30 minutes
Cooking Time: 20 minutes
Servings: 4
Ingredients:
- 1 tbsp flax seed powder + 3 tbsp water
- 2/3 lb crumble tofu
- 1 tbsp quick-cooking oats
- 1 tbsp toasted almond flour
- ½ tsp garlic powder
- ½ tsp onion powder
- Salt and black pepper to taste
- ¼ tsp curry powder
- 3 tbsp whole-grain breadcrumbs
- 4 whole-wheat burger buns, halved

Directions:
1. In a small bowl, mix the flax seed powder with water and allow thickening for 5 minutes to make the flax egg. Set aside.

2. In a medium bowl, mix the tofu, oats, almond flour, garlic powder, onion powder, salt, black pepper, and curry powder. Mold 4 patties out of the mixture and lightly brush both sides with the flax egg.
3. Pour the breadcrumbs onto a plate and coat the patties in the crumbs until well covered.
4. Heat a pan to medium heat and grease well with cooking spray.
5. Cook the patties on both sides until crispy, golden brown and cooked through, 10 minutes.
6. Place each patty between each burger bun and top with the guacamole.
7. Serve immediately.

Nutrition:
- Calories 238
- Fats 15.8 g
- Carbs 14.8 g
- Protein 14.1 g

61. Green Bean and Mushroom Biryani

Preparation Time: 15-30 minutes
Cooking Time: 50 minutes
Servings: 4

Ingredients:
- 1 cup brown rice
- 2 cups water
- Salt to taste
- 3 tbsp plant butter
- 3 medium white onions, chopped
- 6 garlic cloves, minced
- 1 tsp ginger puree
- 1 tbsp turmeric powder + more for dusting
- ¼ tsp cinnamon powder
- 2 tsp garam masala
- ½ tsp cardamom powder
- ½ tsp cayenne powder
- ½ tsp cumin powder
- 1 tsp smoked paprika
- 3 large tomatoes, diced
- 2 green chilies, deseeded and minced
- 1 tbsp tomato puree
- 1 cup chopped cremini mushrooms
- 1 cup chopped mustard greens
- 1 cup plant-based yogurt for topping

Directions:
1. Melt the butter in a large pot and sauté the onions until softened, 3 minutes. Mix in the garlic, ginger, turmeric, cardamom powder, garam masala, cardamom powder, cayenne pepper, cumin powder, paprika, and salt. Stir-fry while cooking until fragrant, from 1 to 2 minutes.
2. Stir in the tomatoes, green chili, tomato puree, and mushrooms. Once boiling, mix in the rice and cover with water. Cover the pot and cook over medium heat until the liquid absorbs and the rice is tender, from 15-20 minutes.
3. Open the lid and fluff in the mustard greens and half of the parsley. Dish the food, top with the coconut yogurt, garnish with the remaining parsley and serve warm.

Nutrition:
- Calories 255
- Fats 16.8 g
- Carbs 25.6 g
- Protein 5.8 g

62. Cabbage & Bell Pepper Skillet

Preparation Time: 15-30 minutes
Cooking Time: 30 minutes
Servings: 4
Ingredients:

- 1 can (28 oz) whole plum tomatoes, undrained
- 1 lb crumbled tempeh
- 1 large yellow onion, chopped
- 1 can (8 oz) tomato sauce
- 2 tbsp plain vinegar
- 1 tbsp pure date sugar
- 1 tsp dried mixed herbs
- 3 large tomatoes, chopped
- ½ tsp black pepper
- 1 small head cabbage, thinly sliced
- 1 medium green bell pepper, deseeded and cut into thin strips

Directions:

1. Drain the tomatoes and reserve their liquid. Chop the tomatoes and set them aside.
2. Add the tempeh to a large skillet and cook until brown, 10 minutes. Mix in the onion, tomato sauce, vinegar, date sugar, mixed herbs, and chopped tomatoes. Close the lid and cook until the liquid reduces and the tomato softens for 10 minutes.
3. Stir in the cabbage and bell pepper; cook until softened, 5 minutes.
4. Dish the food and serve with cooked brown rice.

Nutrition:

- Calories 403
- Fats 16.9 g
- Carbs 44.1 g
- Protein 27.3 g

63. Mixed Bean Burgers with Cashew Cheese

Preparation Time: 15-30 minutes
Cooking Time: 30 minutes
Servings: 4
Ingredients:

- 1 (15 oz) can chickpea, drained and rinsed
- 1 (15 oz) can pinto beans, drained and rinsed
- 1 (15 oz) can red kidney beans, drained and rinsed
- 2 tbsp whole-wheat flour
- ¼ cup dried mixed herbs
- ¼ tsp hot sauce
- ½ tsp garlic powder
- Salt and black pepper to taste
- 4 slices cashew cheese
- 4 whole-grain hamburger buns, split
- 4 small lettuce leaves for topping

Directions:

1. In a medium bowl, mash the chickpea, pinto beans, kidney beans and mix in the flour, mixed herbs, hot sauce, garlic powder, salt, and black pepper. Mold 4 patties out of the mixture and set aside.
2. Heat a grill pan to medium heat and lightly grease with cooking spray.
3. Cook the bean patties on both sides until light brown and cooked through, 10 minutes.
4. Lay a cashew cheese slice on each and allow slight melting, 2 minutes.

5. Remove the patties between the burger buns and top with the lettuce and serve warm.

Nutrition:
- Calories 456
- Fats 16.8 g
- Carbs 56.1 g
- Protein 24 g

64. Baked Sweet Potatoes with Corn Salad

Preparation Time: 15-30 minutes
Cooking Time: 35 minutes
Servings: 4
Ingredients:
For the baked sweet potatoes:
- 3 tbsp olive oil
- 4 medium sweet potatoes, peeled and cut into ½-inch cubes
- 2 limes, juiced
- Salt and black pepper to taste
- ¼ tsp cayenne pepper
- 2 scallions, thinly sliced

For the corn salad:
- 1 (15 oz) can sweet corn kernels, drained
- ½ tbsp, plant butter, melted
- 1 large green chili, deseeded and minced
- 1 tsp cumin powder

Directions:
For the baked sweet potatoes:
1. Preheat the oven to 400°F and lightly grease a baking sheet with cooking spray.

2. In a medium bowl, add the sweet potatoes, lime juice, salt, black pepper, and cayenne pepper. Toss well and spread the mixture on the baking sheet. Bake in the oven until the potatoes soften, 20 to 25 minutes.
3. Remove from the oven, transfer to a serving plate, and garnish with the scallions.

For the corn salad:
1. In a medium bowl, mix the corn kernels, butter, green chili, and cumin powder. Serve the sweet potatoes with the corn salad.

Nutrition:
- Calories 372
- Fats 20.7 g
- Carbs 41.7 g
- Protein 8.9 g

65. Cashew Siam Salad

Preparation Time: 10 minutes
Cooking Time: 3 minutes
Servings: 4
Ingredients:
Salad:
- 4 cups baby spinach, rinsed, drained
- ½ cup pickled red cabbage

Dressing:
- 1-inch piece ginger, finely chopped
- 1 tsp. chili garlic paste

- 1 tbsp. soy sauce
- ½ tbsp. rice vinegar
- 1 tbsp. sesame oil
- 3 tbsp. avocado oil

Toppings:
- ½ cup raw cashews, unsalted
- ¼ cup fresh cilantro, chopped

Directions:
1. Put the spinach and red cabbage in a large bowl. Toss to combine and set the salad aside.
2. Toast the cashews in a frying pan over medium-high heat, stirring occasionally until the cashews are golden brown. This should take about 3 minutes. Turn off the heat and set the frying pan aside.
3. Mix all the dressing ingredients in a medium-sized bowl and use a spoon to mix them into a smooth dressing.
4. Pour the dressing over the spinach salad and top with the toasted cashews.
5. Toss the salad to combine all ingredients and transfer the large bowl to the fridge. Allow the salad to chill for up to one hour – doing so will guarantee a better flavor. Alternatively, the salad can be served right away, topped with the optional cilantro. Enjoy!

Nutrition:
- Calories 236
- Carbohydrates 6.1 g
- Fats 21.6 g
- Protein 4.2 g

66.   Avocado   and Cauliflower Hummus

Preparation Time: 5 minutes
Cooking Time: 25 minutes
Servings: 2
Ingredients:
- 1 medium cauliflower, stem removed and chopped
- 1 large Hass avocado, peeled, pitted, and chopped
- ¼ cup extra virgin olive oil
- 2 garlic cloves
- ½ tbsp. lemon juice
- ½ tsp. onion powder
- Sea salt and ground black pepper to taste
- 2 large carrots
- ¼ cup fresh cilantro, chopped

Directions:
1. Preheat the oven to 450°F, and line a baking tray with aluminum foil.
2. Put the chopped cauliflower on the baking tray and drizzle with 2 tablespoons of olive oil.
3. Roast the chopped cauliflower in the oven for 20-25 minutes, until lightly brown.
4. Remove the tray from the oven and allow the cauliflower to cool down.
5. Add all the ingredients—except the carrots and optional fresh cilantro—to a food processor or blender, and blend the ingredients into a smooth hummus.
6. Transfer the hummus to a medium-sized bowl, cover it and put it in the fridge for at least 30 minutes.
7. Take the hummus out of the fridge and, if desired, top it with the optional chopped cilantro and more salt and pepper to taste; serve with the carrot fries, and enjoy!

Nutrition:
- Calories 416
- Carbohydrates 8.4 g
- Fats 40.3 g
- Protein 3.3 g

67. Raw Zoodles with Avocado 'N Nuts

Preparation Time: 10 minutes
Cooking Time: 3-30 minutes
Servings: 2
Ingredients:
- 1 medium zucchini
- 1½ cups basil
- 1/3 cup water
- 5 tbsp. pine nuts
- 2 tbsp. lemon juice
- 1 medium avocado, peeled, pitted, sliced
- Optional: 2 tbsp. olive oil
- 6 yellow cherry tomatoes, halved
- Optional: 6 red cherry tomatoes, halved
- Sea salt and black pepper to taste

Directions:
1. Add the basil, water, nuts, lemon juice, avocado slices, optional olive oil (if desired), salt, and pepper to a blender.
2. Blend the ingredients into a smooth mixture. Add more salt and pepper to taste and blend again.
3. Divide the sauce and the zucchini noodles between two medium-sized bowls for serving, and combine in each.
4. Top the mixtures with the halved yellow cherry tomatoes and the optional red cherry tomatoes (if desired); serve and enjoy!

Nutrition:
- Calories 317
- Carbohydrates 7.4 g
- Fats 28.1 g
- Protein 7.2 g

68. Cauliflower Sushi

Preparation Time: 30 minutes
Cooking Time: 3-30 minutes
Servings: 4
Ingredients:
Sushi Base:
- 6 cups cauliflower florets
- ½ cup vegan cheese
- 1 medium spring onion, diced
- 4 nori sheets
- Sea salt and pepper to taste
- 1 tbsp. rice vinegar or sushi vinegar
- 1 medium garlic clove, minced

Filling:
- 1 medium Hass avocado, peeled, sliced
- ½ medium cucumber, skinned, sliced
- 4 asparagus spears
- A handful of enoki mushrooms

Directions:
1. Put the cauliflower florets in a food processor or blender. Pulse the florets into a rice-like substance. When using readymade cauliflower rice, add this to the blender.
2. Add the vegan cheese, spring onions, and vinegar to the food processor or blender. Top these ingredients with salt and pepper to taste, and pulse everything into a chunky mixture. Make sure not to turn the ingredients into a puree by pulsing too long.
3. Taste and add more vinegar, salt, or pepper to taste. Add the optional minced garlic clove to the blender and pulse again for a few seconds.
4. Lay out the nori sheets and spread the cauliflower rice mixture out evenly between

the sheets. Make sure to leave at least 2 inches of the top and bottom edges empty.

5. Place one or more combinations of multiple filling ingredients along the center of the spread-out rice mixture. Experiment with different ingredients per nori sheet for the best flavor.
6. Roll up each nori sheet tightly. (Using a sushi mat will make this easier.)
7. Either serve the sushi as a nori roll or, slice each roll up into sushi pieces.
8. Serve right away with a small amount of wasabi, pickled ginger, and soy sauce!

Nutrition:
- Calories 189
- Carbohydrates 7.6 g
- Fats 14.4 g
- Protein 6.1 g

69. Spinach and Mashed Tofu Salad

Preparation Time: 20 minutes
Cooking Time: 3-30 minutes
Servings: 4
Ingredients:
- 2-8 oz. blocks firm tofu, drained
- 4 cups baby spinach leaves
- 4 tbsp. cashew butter
- 1½ tbsp. soy sauce
- 1-inch piece ginger, finely chopped
- 1 tsp. red miso paste
- 2 tbsp. sesame seeds
- 1 tsp. organic orange zest
- 1 tsp. nori flakes
- 2 tbsp. water

Directions:
1. Use paper towels to absorb any excess water left in the tofu before crumbling both blocks into small pieces.
2. In a large bowl, combine the mashed tofu with the spinach leaves.
3. Mix the remaining ingredients in another small bowl and, if desired, add the optional water for a more smooth dressing.
4. Pour this dressing over the mashed tofu and spinach leaves.
5. Transfer the bowl to the fridge and allow the salad to chill for up to one hour. Doing so will guarantee a better flavor. Or, the salad can be served right away. Enjoy!

Nutrition:
- Calories 166
- Carbohydrates 5.5 g
-
- Fats 10.7 g
- Protein 11.3 g

70. Cucumber Edamame Salad

Preparation Time: 5 minutes
Cooking Time: 8 minutes
Servings: 2
Ingredients:

- 3 tbsp. avocado oil
- 1 cup cucumber, sliced into thin rounds
- ½ cup fresh sugar snap peas, sliced or whole
- ½ cup fresh edamame
- ¼ cup radish, sliced
- 1 large Hass avocado, peeled, pitted, sliced
- 1 nori sheet, crumbled
- 2 tsp. roasted sesame seeds
- 1 tsp. salt

Directions:

1. Bring a medium-sized pot filled halfway with water to a boil over medium-high heat.
2. Add the sugar snaps and cook them for about 2 minutes.
3. Take the pot off the heat, drain the excess water, transfer the sugar snaps to a medium-sized bowl and set them aside for now.
4. Fill the pot with water again, add the teaspoon of salt and bring to a boil over medium-high heat.
5. Add the edamame to the pot and let them cook for about 6 minutes.
6. Take the pot off the heat, drain the excess water, transfer the soybeans to the bowl with sugar snaps and let them cool down for about 5 minutes.
7. Combine all ingredients, except the nori crumbs and roasted sesame seeds, in a medium-sized bowl.
8. Carefully stir, using a spoon, until all ingredients are evenly coated in oil.
9. Top the salad with the nori crumbs and roasted sesame seeds.
10. Transfer the bowl to the fridge and allow the salad to cool for at least 30 minutes. Serve chilled and enjoy!

Nutrition:

- Calories 409
- Carbohydrates 7.1 g
- Fats 38.25 g
- Protein 7.6 g

Chapter 4. Desserts

71. Salted Caramel Chocolate Cups

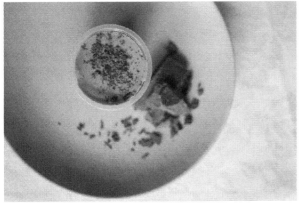

Preparation Time: 5 minutes
Cooking Time: 2 minutes
Servings: 12
Ingredients:
- ¼ teaspoon sea salt granules
- 1 cup dark chocolate chips, unsweetened
- 2 teaspoons coconut oil
- 6 tablespoons caramel sauce

Directions:
1. Take a heatproof bowl, add chocolate chips and oil, stir until mixed, then microwave for 1 minute until melted, stir chocolate and continue heating in the microwave for 30 seconds.
2. Take twelve mini muffin tins, line them with muffin liners, spoon a little bit of chocolate mixture into the tins, spread the chocolate in the bottom and along the sides, and freeze for 10 minutes until set.
3. Then fill each cup with ½ tablespoon of caramel sauce, cover with remaining chocolate and freeze for another 20 minutes until set.
4. When ready to eat, peel off liner from the cup, sprinkle with sauce, and serve.

Nutrition:
- Calories 80
- Fat 5 g
- Carbs 10 g
- Protein 1 g
- Fiber 0.5 g

72. Chocolate Peanut Butter Energy Bites

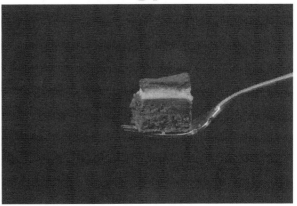

Preparation Time: 1 hour and 5 minutes
Cooking Time: 0 minute
Servings: 4
Ingredients:
- 1/2 cup oats, old-fashioned
- 1/3 cup cocoa powder, unsweetened
- 1 cup dates, chopped
- 1/2 cup shredded coconut flakes, unsweetened
- 1/2 cup peanut butter

Directions:
1. Place oats in a food processor along with dates and pulse for 1 minute until the paste starts to come together.
2. Then add remaining ingredients, and blend until incorporated and very thick mixture comes together.
3. Shape the mixture into balls, refrigerate for 1 hour until set and then serve.

Nutrition:
- Calories 88.6
- Fat 5 g
- Carbs 10 g
- Protein 2.3 g
- Fiber 1.6 g

73. Mango Coconut Cheesecake

Preparation Time: 4 hours and 10 minutes
Cooking Time: 0 minute
Servings: 4
Ingredients:
For the Crust:
- 1 cup macadamia nuts
- 1 cup dates, pitted, soaked in hot water for 10 minutes

For the Filling:
- 2 cups cashews, soaked in warm water for 10 minutes
- 1/2 cup and 1 tablespoon maple syrup
- 1/3 cup and 2 tablespoons coconut oil
- 1/4 cup lemon juice
- 1/2 cup and 2 tablespoons coconut milk, unsweetened, chilled

For the Topping:
- 1 cup fresh mango slices

Directions:
1. Prepare the crust, and for this, place nuts in a food processor and process until mixture resembles crumbs.
2. Drain the dates, add them to the food processor and blend for 2 minutes until thick mixture comes together.
3. Take a 4-inch cheesecake pan, place date mixture in it, spread and press evenly, and set aside.
4. Prepare the filling and for this, place all its ingredients in a food processor and blend for 3 minutes until smooth.
5. Pour the filling into the crust, spread evenly, and then freeze for 4 hours until set.
6. Top the cake with mango slices and then serve.

Nutrition:
- Calories 200
- Fat 11 g
- Carbs 22.5 g
- Protein 2 g
- Fiber 1 g

74. Mixed Nut Chocolate Fudge

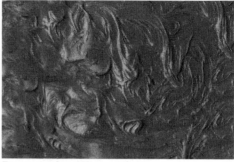

Preparation Time: 15-30 minutes
Cooking Time: 2 hours 10 minutes
Servings: 4
Ingredients:
- 3 cups unsweetened chocolate chips
- ¼ cup thick coconut milk
- 1 ½ tsp vanilla extract
- A pinch salt
- 1 cup chopped mixed nuts

Directions:
1. Line a 9-inch square pan with baking paper and set it aside.
2. Melt the chocolate chips, coconut milk, and vanilla in a medium pot over low heat.
3. Mix in the salt and nuts until well distributed and pour the mixture into the square pan.
4. Refrigerate for at least 2 hours.
5. Remove from the fridge, cut into squares and serve.

Nutrition:
- Calories 907
- Fats 31.5 g
- Carbs 152.1 g
- Protein 7.7 g

75. Date Cake Slices

Preparation Time: 15-30 minutes
Cooking Time: 1 hour 20 minutes
Servings: 4
Ingredients:

- ½ cup cold plant butter, cut in pieces, plus extra for greasing
- 1 tbsp flax seed powder + 3 tbsp water
- ½ cup whole-wheat flour, plus extra for dusting
- ¼ cup chopped pecans and walnuts
- 1 tsp baking powder
- 1 tsp baking soda
- 1 tsp cinnamon powder
- 1 tsp salt
- 1/3 cup water
- 1/3 cup pitted dates, chopped
- ½ cup pure date sugar
- 1 tsp vanilla extract
- ¼ cup pure date syrup for drizzling.

Directions:

1. Preheat the oven to 350°F and lightly grease a round baking dish with some plant butter.
2. In a small bowl, mix the flax seed powder with water and allow thickening for 5 minutes to make the flax egg.
3. In a food processor, add the flour, nuts, baking powder, baking soda, cinnamon powder, and salt. Blend until well combined.
4. Add the water, dates, date sugar, and vanilla. Process until smooth with tiny pieces of dates evident.
5. Pour the batter into the baking dish and bake in the oven for 1 hour and 10 minutes or until a toothpick inserted comes out clean.

Remove the dish from the oven, invert the cake onto a serving platter to cool, drizzle with the date syrup, slice, and serve.

Nutrition:

- Calories 850
- Fats 61.2 g
- Carbs 65.7 g
- Protein 12.8 g

76. Chocolate Mousse Cake

Preparation Time: 15-30 minutes
Cooking Time: 40 minutes + 6 hours 30 minutes chilling
Servings: 4
Ingredients:

- 2/3 cup toasted almond flour
- ¼ cup unsalted plant butter, melted
- 2 cups unsweetened chocolate bars, broken into pieces
- 2 ½ cups coconut cream
- Fresh raspberries or strawberries for topping

Directions:

1. Lightly grease a 9-inch springform pan with some plant butter and set it aside.
2. Mix the almond flour and plant butter in a medium bowl and pour the mixture into the springform pan. Use the spoon to spread and press the mixture into the bottom of the pan. Place in the refrigerator to firm for 30 minutes.

3. Meanwhile, pour the chocolate in a safe microwave bowl and melt for 1 minute stirring every 30 seconds.
4. Remove from the microwave and mix in the coconut cream and maple syrup.
5. Remove the cake pan from the oven, pour the chocolate mixture on top, making sure to shake the pan and even the layer. Chill further for 4 to 6 hours.
6. Take out the pan from the fridge, release the cake and garnish with the raspberries or strawberries.
7. Slice and serve.

Nutrition:
- Calories 608
- Fats 60.5 g
- Carbs 19.8 g
- Protein 6.3 g

77. Chocolate & Pistachio Popsicles

Preparation Time: 15-30 minutes
Cooking Time: 5 minutes + 3 hours chilling
Servings: 4

Ingredients:
- ½ cup unsweetened chocolate chips, melted
- 1 ½ cups oat milk
- 1 tbsp unsweetened cocoa powder
- 3 tbsp pure date syrup
- 1 tsp vanilla extract
- A handful pistachios, chopped

Directions:
1. In a blender, add chocolate, oat milk, cocoa powder, date syrup, vanilla, pistachios, and process until smooth. Divide the mixture into popsicle molds and freeze for 3 hours.
2. Dip the popsicle molds in warm water to loosen the popsicles and pull out the popsicles.

Nutrition:
- Calories 315
- Fats 17.8 g
- Carbs 34.9 g
- Protein 11.9 g

78. Strawberry Cupcakes with Cashew Cheese Frosting

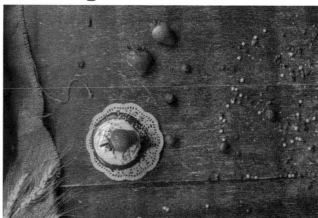

Preparation Time: 15-30 minutes
Cooking Time: 35 minutes + 30 minutes chilling
Servings: 4
Ingredients:
For the cupcakes:
- 2 cups whole-wheat flour
- ¼ cup cornstarch
- 2 ½ tsp baking powder

58

- 1 ½ cups pure date sugar
- ½ tsp salt
- ¾ cup unsalted plant butter, room temperature
- 3 tsp vanilla extract
- 1 cup strawberries, pureed
- 1 cup oat milk, room temperature

For the frosting:
- ¾ cup cashew cream
- 2 tbsp coconut oil, melted
- 3 tbsp pure maple syrup
- 1 tsp vanilla extract
- 1 tsp freshly squeezed lemon juice
- ¼ tsp salt
- 2-4 tbsp water as needed for blending

Directions:
1. Preheat the oven to 350°F and line a 12-holed muffin tray with cupcake liners. Set aside.
2. In a large bowl, mix the flour, cornstarch, baking powder, date sugar, and salt.
3. Using an electric mixer, whisk in the plant butter, vanilla extract, strawberries, and oat milk until well combined.
4. Divide the mixture into the muffin cups two-thirds way up and bake in the oven for 20 to 25 minutes or until golden brown on top and a toothpick inserted comes out clean. Remove the cupcakes and allow cooling while you make the frosting.
5. In a blender, add the cashew cream, coconut oil, maple syrup, vanilla, lemon juice, and salt. Process until smooth. If the mixture is too thick, add some water to lighten the consistency a little. Pour the frosting into medium and chill for 30 minutes.
6. Transfer the mixture into a piping bag and swirl mounds of the frosting onto the cupcakes. Serve immediately.

Nutrition:
- Calories 853
- Fats 42 g
- Carbs 112.8 g
- Protein 14.3 g

79. Nut Stuffed Sweet Apples

Preparation Time: 15-30 minutes
Cooking Time: 35 minutes
Servings: 4
Ingredients:
- 4 gala apples
- 3 tbsp pure maple syrup
- 4 tbsp almond flour
- 6 tbsp pure date sugar
- 6 tbsp plant butter, cold and cubed
- 1 cup chopped mixed nuts

Directions:
1. Preheat the oven the 400°F.
2. Slice off the top of the apples and use a melon baller or spoon to scoop out the cores of the apples. In a bowl, mix the maple syrup, almond flour, date sugar, butter, and nuts.
3. Spoon the mixture into the apples and then bake in the oven for 25 minutes or until the nuts are golden brown on top and the apples soft. Remove the apples from the oven, allow cooling, and serve.

Nutrition:
- Calories 581
- Fats 43.6 g
- Carbs 52.1 g
- Protein 3.6 g

80. Classic Pecan Pie

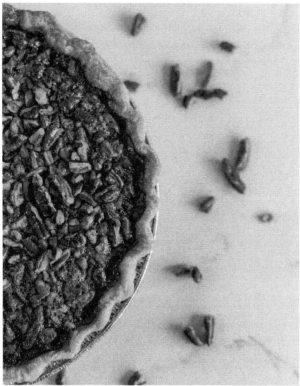

Preparation Time: 15-30 minutes
Cooking Time: 50 minutes + 1-hour chilling
Servings: 4
Ingredients:
For the piecrust:
- 4 tbsp flax seed powder + 12 tbsp water
- 1/3 cup whole-wheat flour + more for dusting
- ½ tsp salt
- ¼ cup plant butter, cold and crumbled
- 3 tbsp pure malt syrup
- 1 ½ tsp vanilla extract
For the filling:
- 3 tbsp flax seed powder + 9 tbsp water
- 2 cups toasted pecans, coarsely chopped
- 1 cup light corn syrup
- ½ cup pure date sugar
- 1 tbsp pure pomegranate molasses
- 4 tbsp plant butter, melted
- ½ tsp salt
- 2 tsp vanilla extract

Directions:
1. Preheat the oven to 350°F and grease a large pie pan with cooking spray.
2. In a medium bowl, mix the flax seed powder with water and allow thickening for 5 minutes. Do this for the filling's flax egg, too, in a separate bowl.
3. In a large bowl, combine the flour and salt. Add the plant butter, and using an electric hand mixer, whisk until crumbly, pour in the crust's flax egg, maple syrup, vanilla, and mix until smooth dough forms.
4. Flatten the dough on a flat surface, cover with plastic wrap, and refrigerate for 1 hour.
5. After, lightly dust a working surface with flour, remove the dough onto the surface, and using a rolling pin, flatten the dough into a 1-inch diameter circle.
6. Lay the dough on the pie pan and press to fit the shape of the pan. Use a knife to trim the edges of the pan. Lay a parchment paper on the dough, pour on some baking beans and bake in the oven until golden brown, 15 to 20 minutes. Remove the pan from the oven, pour out the baking beans, and allow cooling.
7. In a large bowl, mix the filling's flax egg, pecans, corn syrup, date sugar, pomegranate molasses, plant butter, salt, and vanilla. Pour and spread the mixture on the piecrust. Bake further for 20 minutes or until the filling sets. Remove from the oven, decorate with more pecans, slice, and cool. Slice and serve.

Nutrition:
- Calories 992
- Fats 59.8 g
- Carbs 117.6 g
- Protein 8 g

81. Asian Fruit Salad

Preparation Time: 30 minutes
Cooking Time: 0 minutes
Servings: 8
Ingredients:

- Passion fruit, one-half cup (about six of the fruit)
- Papaya, one chopped
- Pineapple, one cup chunked
- Oranges, two separated into segments
- Star fruit, three sliced thin
- Mangoes, two large, peeled and chunked
- Mint, fresh, one-third cup chopped coarse
- Lime juice, one third cup
- Lime zest, one tablespoon
- Ginger, ground, one tablespoon
- Vanilla extract, one tablespoon
- Brown sugar, one half cup
- Water, four cups

Directions:

1. Mix the water and the sugar in a medium-sized saucepan and put it over medium to high heat until the sugar is dissolved.
2. Let this simmer for five minutes over very low heat, so the sugar does not burn. Add in the vanilla extract and the ginger and stir well.
3. Let this cook for ten more minutes. Let the mix cool off the heat until it is room temperature, and then add in the mint, juice, and zest.
4. During the time the sauce is cooling, mix the remainder of the Ingredients in a large-sized bowl.
5. Pour the syrup mixture over the fruit in the bowl and mix gently to coat all pieces with the sauce.
6. Put the bowl in the refrigerator until the fruit is cold, then serve.

Nutrition:

- Calories 220
- Protein 3 g
- Fat 1 g
- Carbs 56 g

82. Mimosa Salad

Preparation Time: 10 minutes
Cooking Time: 0 minutes
Servings: 8
Ingredients:

- Mint, fresh, one half cup
- Orange juice, one half cup
- Pineapple, one cup cut into small pieces
- Strawberries, one cup cut into quarters
- Blueberries, one cup
- Blackberries, one cup
- Kiwi, three peeled and sliced

Directions:

1. In a large-sized bowl, mix all of the fruits and then top with the orange juice and the fresh mint.
2. Toss gently together all of the fruit until they are well mixed.

Nutrition:

- Calories 215
- Protein 3 g
- Fat 1 g
- Carbs 49 g

83. Key Lime Pie

Preparation Time: 3 hours and 15 minutes
Cooking Time: 0 minute
Servings: 12
Ingredients:
For the Crust:
- ¾ cup coconut flakes, unsweetened
- 1 cup dates, soaked in warm water for 10 minutes in water, drained

For the Filling:
- ¾ cup of coconut meat
- 1 ½ avocado, peeled, pitted
- 2 tablespoons key lime juice
- ¼ cup agave

Directions:
1. Prepare the crust, and for this, place all its ingredients in a food processor and pulse for 3 to 5 minutes until the thick paste comes together.
2. Take an 8-inch pie pan, grease it with oil, pour crust mixture in it and spread and press the mixture evenly in the bottom and along the sides, and freeze until required.
3. Prepare the filling and for this, place all its ingredients in a food processor, and pulse for 2 minutes until smooth.
4. Pour the filling into the prepared pan, smooth the top, and freeze for 3 hours until set.
5. Cut pie into slices and then serve.

Nutrition:
- Calories 213
- Fat 10 g
- Carbs 29 g
- Protein 1200 g
- Fiber 6 g

84.   Chocolate   Mint Grasshopper Pie

Preparation Time: 4 hours and 15 minutes
Cooking Time: 0 minute
Servings: 4
Ingredients:
For the Crust:
- 1 cup dates, soaked in warm water for 10 minutes in water, drained
- 1/8 teaspoons salt
- 1/2 cup pecans
- 1 teaspoons cinnamon
- 1/2 cup walnuts

For the Filling:
- ½ cup mint leaves
- 2 cups of cashews, soaked in warm water for 10 minutes in water, drained
- 2 tablespoons coconut oil
- 1/4 cup and 2 tablespoons of agave
- 1/4 teaspoons spirulina
- 1/4 cup water

Directions:
1. Prepare the crust, and for this, place all its ingredients in a food processor and pulse for 3 to 5 minutes until the thick paste comes together.
2. Take a 6-inch springform pan, grease it with oil, place crust mixture in it and spread and

press the mixture evenly in the bottom and along the sides, and freeze until required.
3. Prepare the filling and for this, place all its ingredients in a food processor, and pulse for 2 minutes until smooth.
4. Pour the filling into the prepared pan, smooth the top, and freeze for 4 hours until set.
5. Cut pie into slices and then serve.

Nutrition:
- Calories 223.7
- Fat 7.5 g
- Carbs 36 g
- Protein 2.5 g
- Fiber 1 g

Chapter 5. 30-Day Meal Plan

Day	Breakfast	Lunch	Dinner	Dinner
1	Berry Cream Compote Over Crepes	Cheesy Creamy Farfalline	Raw Zoodles with Avocado 'N Nuts	Salted Caramel Chocolate Cups
2	Mixed Berry Walnut Yogurt	Basil Pesto Mushrooms Pasta	Cashew Siam Salad	Chocolate & Pistachio Popsicles
3	Orange Butter Crepes	Smoked Tofu and Cherry Tomatoes	Cucumber Edamame Salad	Chocolate Peanut Butter Energy Bites
4	Creole Tofu Scramble	Spaghetti Squash with Mushroom Sauce Pasta	Spinach and Mashed Tofu Salad	Nut Stuffed Sweet Apples
5	High Protein Toast	Creamy Tofu Marsala Pasta	Baked Sweet Potatoes With Corn Salad	Mango Coconut Cheesecake
6	Berry Compote Pancakes	Creamy Penne with Vegetables	Cauliflower Sushi	Classic Pecan Pie
7	Carrot And Chocolate Bread	Basil Spaghetti Pasta	Simply Kale Lasagna	Mixed Nut Chocolate Fudge

8	Savory Breakfast Salad	Fresh Tomato Mint Pasta	Creamy Fettucine With Peas	Asian Fruit Salad
9	Apple Cinnamon Muffins	Easy Spinach Ricotta Pasta	Buckwheat Cabbage Rolls	Date Cake Slices
10	Guacamole	Zucchini Noodles	Bbq Black Bean Burgers	Mimosa Salad
11	Pineapple French Toasts	Classic Goulash	Crispy Tofu Burgers	Classic Pecan Pie
12	Almond Plum Oats Overnight	Cabbage and Noodles	Crispy Tofu Burgers	Chocolate Mousse Cake
13	Almond Waffles With Cranberries	Pasta with Peppers	Paprika & Tomato Pasta Primavera	Mimosa Salad
14	Sweet Coconut Raspberry Pancakes	Fresh Tomato Mint Pasta	Grilled Zucchini And Spinach Pizza	Chocolate & Pistachio Popsicles
15	Pumpkin-Pistachio Tea Cake	Creamy Spinach Artichoke Pasta	Green Bean And Mushroom Biryani	Salted Caramel Chocolate Cups

16	Mushroom Avocado Panini	Easy Spinach Ricotta Pasta	Cannellini Beans Bow Ties	Strawberry Cupcakes With Cashew Cheese Frosting
17	Nectarine Chia Pudding	Roasted Red Pepper Pasta	Baked Sweet Potatoes With Corn Salad	Nut Stuffed Sweet Apples
18	Southwest Breakfast Bowl	Creamy Mushroom Herb Pasta	Zucchini Rolls In Tomato Sauce	Nut Stuffed Sweet Apples
19	Irish Brown Bread	Pasta with Eggplant Sauce	Mixed Bean Burgers With Cashew Cheese	Strawberry Cupcakes With Cashew Cheese Frosting
20	Pimiento Cheese Breakfast Biscuits	Parsley Hummus Pasta	White Bean Stuffed Squash	Classic Pecan Pie
21	Chickpea Omelet With Spinach And Mushrooms	Cabbage and Noodles	Cabbage & Bell Pepper Skillet	Asian Fruit Salad
22	Raspberry Raisin Muffins With Orange Glaze	Basil Spaghetti Pasta	Cashew Siam Salad	Asian Fruit Salad

23	Vegan Muffins Breakfast Sandwich	Corn and Chiles Fusilli	Avocado and Cauliflower Hummus	Chocolate & Pistachio Popsicles
24	Berry Cream Compote Over Crepes	Lemon Garlic Broccoli Macaroni	Bbq Black Bean Burgers	Mimosa Salad
25	Guacamole	Classic Goulash	Mozzarella Lemon Pasta	Salted Caramel Chocolate Cups
26	Nectarine Chia Pudding	Basil-Coconut Peas and Broccoli	Green Goddess Pasta	Chocolate Mousse Cake
27	Mushroom Avocado Panini	Pasta Puttanesca	Grilled Tempeh With Green Beans	Chocolate Peanut Butter Energy Bites
28	Mixed Berry Walnut Yogurt	Zucchini Noodles	Creamy Fettucine With Peas	Date Cake Slices
29	Apple Cinnamon Muffins	Lemon Parsley Pasta	Simply Kale Lasagna	Mango Coconut Cheesecake

30	Southwest Breakfast Bowl	Kale Lasagna Roll-Ups	Buckwheat Cabbage Rolls	Mixed Nut Chocolate Fudge

Conclusion

There are so many powerful and persuasive reasons to make a positive change and switch over to a plant-based diet. It will improve your quality of life, give you more energy and vitality, help you lose unwanted body fat, and it may even lengthen your years on this beautiful planet. As a bonus, by making the change, you will be making a real and significant difference to our planet Earth's future. So much energy and fossil fuels are wasted by sourcing meat and other animal products, transporting them from place to place across miles and miles of road, and processing all of these animal products.

On top of that, there is an enormous crisis of animals being treated extremely inhumanely and cruelly. In order to mass-produce meat and animal products to meet the enormous demand of the market, many manufacturers put animal comfort and quality of life last and do not make it a priority to treat them humanely and ethically.

There is also an incredible amount of food waste that happens in the production and processing of animal products. Extraordinary amounts of energy and resources are expended, and too much gets simply thrown away. By switching to a plant-based diet, you will be greatly decreasing your carbon footprint and ensuring that fewer animals have to suffer at the hands of humans. And isn't that a good feeling?

Considering all the ethical reasons for switching to a plant-based diet, the enormous health benefits and improved quality of life are the icings on an already extremely appealing cake.

Thank you for reading!

Printed in Great Britain
by Amazon